# THE TIES THAT BIND

# Books by Joyce A. Ladner

*Tomorrow's Tomorrow: The Black Woman*

*Death of White Sociology*

*Adolescence and Poverty: Challenge for the 1990's*
(edited with Peter Edelman)

*Selected Papers from the Proceedings of the*
*Conference on Ethics, Higher Education*
*and Social Responsibility*
(with Segun Gbadesgesin)

*Mixed Families:*
*Adopting Across Racial Boundaries*

*Lives of Promise, Lives of Pain:*
*Young Mothers After New Change*
(with Janet C. Quint and Judith S. Musick, forthcoming)

# THE TIES THAT BIND

## Timeless Values
for
African American Families

JOYCE A. LADNER, PH.D.

John Wiley & Sons, Inc.
New York • Chichester • Weinheim • Brisbane
Singapore • Toronto

AAM0429

FREE PUBLIC LIBRARY
TRENTON N.J.

This book is printed on acid-free paper. ♾

Copyright © 1998 by Joyce A. Ladner. All rights reserved.
Published by John Wiley & Sons, Inc.
Published simultaneously in Canada.
Design and production by Navta Associates, Inc.

No part of this publication may be reproduced, stored in a retrieval system or transmitted in any form or by any means, electronic, mechanical, photocopying, recording, scanning or otherwise, except as permitted under Sections 107 or 108 of the 1976 United States Copyright Act, without either the prior written permission of the Publisher or authorization through payment of the appropriate per-copy fee to the Copyright Clearance Center, 222 Rosewood Drive, Danvers, MA 01923, (978) 750-8400, fax (978) 750-4744. Requests to the Publisher for permission should be addressed to the Permissions Department, John Wiley & Sons, Inc., 605 Third Avenue, New York, NY 10158-0012, (212) 850-6011, fax (212) 850-6008, E-Mail: PERMREQ @ WILEY.COM.

This publication is designed to provide accurate and authoritative information in regard to the subject matter covered. It is sold with the understanding that the publisher is not engaged in rendering professional services. If professional advice or other expert assistance is required, the services of a competent professional person should be sought.

***Library of Congress Cataloging-in-Publication Data:***

Ladner, Joyce A.
The ties that bind : timeless values for African American families / Joyce A. Ladner.
p. cm.
Includes bibliographical references (p. ) and index.
ISBN 0–471–19953–2 (acid-free paper)
1. Afro-American families. 2. Social values—United States.
3. Afro-Americans—Conduct of life. I. Title.
E185.86.L335 1998
306.85'089'96073—dc21 98–38571

Printed in the United States of America

10 9 8 7 6 5 4 3 2 1

*To the memory of my dear mother,*

*Annie Ruth Perryman,*

*whose values guided every stage*

*of the development of my life.*

*To my son,*

*Thomas Ladner Carrington,*

*in whom these values will be*

*manifest in the next generation.*

# CONTENTS

# 2
# THE BLACK VALUE SYSTEM—TIMELESS TIES THAT BIND

# 3

# PERSONAL TRANSITIONS— THE POWER OF INTIMATE TIES

# 4

## PASSING ON THE LEGACY

# FOREWORD

## By Dr. Dorothy I. Height

T here was never a time when life was simple and it was easy to chart the right course. For African American families, in particular, life has always been full of unique challenges. Yet, guided by their traditional values, generations of African Americans have nurtured children into being strong, productive adults. And so can you, despite the complexity of modern life and the difficult choices our children face.

*The Ties That Bind* points the way. Powerful and comprehensive, this book is a major contribution to our understanding of the reasons why black families have not only endured, but excelled. This book confirms that when traditional values gave us direction, we were clear about right and wrong. It forcefully reminds us that when our communities were serious about the survival of the race, certain critical values consistently enriched our churches, schools, and social, fraternal, and civic organizations. As a result, children quickly developed a positive sense of community and identity.

Forged from our original needs as a people, those values have endured. Today, they form a culture that still unites African Americans across occupations, income, geography, and time. Reading this book, black families can identify those values; develop a renewed respect for their heritage; and discover scores of ways to share its joys, rewards, and important responsibilities with their children and the children of their communities.

Joyce Ladner and I were both shaped by traditional African American values. We grew up more than 30 years apart and in very different places. Yet despite her rural Mississippi and my industrial Pennsylvania backgrounds, we grew up learning the same things. Each of us revered the older people in our families and listened to their stories with rapt attention and respect. Storytelling was both an art form and a way to teach us lessons about integrity and self-identity.

We were both "church-girls" growing up in families who rarely missed a Sunday service. Family church attendance was supplemented by choir practice, Bible study, and a host of other social, political, and civic activities in the church.

Joyce and I have worked all our lives, beginning as children. We worked hard in school to be good students. Education was a vital part of life. We knew we had to learn all we could, to take advantage of every opportunity to help our teachers and our peers. We worked hard at home doing chores and helping neighbors. It was a privilege for a child to go to the store or to run an errand for an adult. It gave the child a chance to be honest by bringing back the correct change. It gave the child a chance to take pride in building a good name by demonstrating responsibility.

What Joyce and I learned as children about traditional African American values is echoed in *The Ties That Bind* and illustrated by the National Council of Negro Women's annual Black Family Reunion. It is time to bring those same lessons about values to new generations of African American children. Here is a much-needed, authentic road map.

Returning to our traditional African American values is the best way for us to put aside our fears about the future. This wise and spirited book speaks out loud about what we believe about respect for others, resilience, self-reliance, and resourcefulness. It will enable you to share the great lessons of the past with your children and guide them to a stronger, more positive future.

# ACKNOWLEDGMENTS

$\int$cholars are supposed to be dispassionate about their subject matter. We are expected to exclude our personal experiences and values from the sacred realm of ideas. Otherwise we run the risk of having our work devalued because critics may think we have violated the code of "objective" scientific inquiry. But I see things differently, and I am willing to take the risk.

The real issue is not whether we hold personal biases but whether we have been able to put them in the proper perspective; whether we have been honest with ourselves and our readers, and acknowledged what these biases are. So before I begin this book there are several personal things I want to make plain.

First, I am a product of the segregated South and of the civil rights movement. Through the accident of history,

I was a college student in my home state of Mississippi when the movement hit that most racist of all states. I was propelled into the middle of the most important social movement of the century. The years 1960 to 1964, which coincided with my college days, were the most exciting of my life. The movement bred hope and inspiration for a better, if not a perfect, society. In my youthful mind I was sure that freedom was only a couple of years away and centuries of wrongs would be righted.

I was naïve yet the eternal optimist. As the years passed, it became clear that many of those who fought the hardest for their rights were least likely to reap the benefits from the rewards. Thus this book is born of a sense of frustration. What happened to our values? To our hopes? How do we inspire and enable every black child to have a better life? Our work is not yet finished.

This book is my answer to these questions, and the product of my soul-searching on the values that the civil rights generation developed while growing up in traditional African American families. Unfettered rules of conduct deeply ingrained in my consciousness from early childhood put me on the road to freedom and prosperity. I was not unique. At one time, most African Americans in every region of the nation received the same kind of "home training" based on the core of values from which these rules had sprung.

This book, therefore, is also the work of my late mother, Annie Ruth Perryman. Without an ounce of uncertainty, she molded me. Being my mother's child meant hearing her homespun wisdom each and every day. Her parables and her golden nuggets of advice were usually on the mark. She had the preternatural ability to cut to the heart of a problem, and to render her verdict on a person's character and upbringing, or lack thereof, in a split second. The older I become, the more I remember these "lessons" of hers. She gave me something that is priceless in today's society. So I want to thank Mother for all she taught me. I hope I have done her views justice. My stepfather, William Perryman, who raised me from the time I was a toddler, taught me the same values as Mother. I am thankful to him for teaching me the old ways.

I could never have completed this book alone. My sisters Dorie Ladner Churnet, Willa Tate, Billie Ruth Collins, and Hazel Mims joined me on Saturday-morning conference calls to discuss the many sides of Mother. We used to tease Mother and her sister Aunt LeDrester, both of whom we called the Hattiesburg American newspaper, because they kept up with all the goings-on in the community. Now that Mother is gone, we five sisters keep the tradition alive, albeit from an orbit that covers Mississippi, Texas, and Washington, D.C., where we live. My brothers also jogged my memory of our growing-up years. I want to thank them—Harvey Garrett, Woodrow Ladner, and Fred and Archie Perryman—for their loving kindness and their patience. Over the years, my mother's sisters and brothers answered many of my questions and provided the context for many of the bits and pieces of conversations I could recall from my childhood. My aunts Oneta Keys, Mary Thompkins, Lucy Mae Johnson, and especially LeDrester Hayes were particularly helpful. Aunt LeDrester and Mother were closest, so Aunt LeDrester had to fill in a lot of the gaps in my knowledge after Mother passed on. My uncles J.P. (Jerry), Lon, Luther, Prince, Joe, and Arthur Neal Woulard taught me more than they realized. Uncles J.P., Luther, and Prince were storehouses of knowledge, and they took great delight in talking about my grandparents, Joe Woulard and Martha Gates Woulard, and all their kith and kin. They were passionate when they talked about family.

I also thank my daddy, Eunice Stafford Ladner, who always lived apart from me because he and Mother divorced when I was a toddler. Most of the Ladners moved away to Chicago and San Francisco when I was only a few years old. Fortunately, starting in my adolescence, summer visits helped me to forge strong bonds with my paternal family. My paternal grandfather, Thomas Ladner, from whom I earned my childhood nickname, Tom, died when I was about two years old. I knew my paternal grandmother, Della Ladner Barrett, well because she lived long enough to see my son, Thomas, her great-grandchild. Daddy, his sister Christine Dixon, and his brother Thomas Fontaine, as well as his brothers Charles and Valois, who are deceased, taught me a lot about my paternal family. To all of them, I am grateful.

To my parents, as well as my aunts and uncles, thank you very much. I hope I have captured what your lives were really like.

My son, Thomas Maigore Ladner Carrington, has been a constant joy and inspiration. Throughout the writing, he inquired often, but never took my offer to read any of the material. He said he wanted to wait until it was in book form. "But what if you don't like what I've written about you?" I asked him. "It's your book, Mom," he said, "and you have the right to say anything you want to about me." I am grateful to God that I have such a trusting child who has brought me much joy.

I owe much to my niece Yodit Mebrat Churnet, who has grown up as my surrogate daughter. In addition to doing a rough edit of the manuscript, she also answered my inquiries about how she viewed our relationship, events that occurred during her childhood, and how she felt about the role I played in raising her. I regret that I did not have as close a relationship with my other six nieces and my four nephews, who grew up in other parts of the country. I wrote this book in part so that they may have some knowledge of their family history.

My sister Dorie Ladner Churnet deserves a lot of credit

for helping me with the family history, which grew out of years of her prodigious genealogical research. She has also coped with the long bouts of mercurial personality that seem to take over my life when I am writing. Dorie continues to play her lifelong role as my alter ego. Thank you, Dorie, for being there.

I want to thank my literary agent, Denise Stinson, for suggesting that I write this book at this time. She was very supportive when it was only the germ of an idea. My editor par excellence, Carole Hall, took my raw material and mined it until everything became clear. She has the gifts of insight and perseverance that were invaluable to this project. Few editors have such a unique ability to get inside an author's head and understand the subject matter from her stance.

I want to thank my colleagues at the Howard University School of Social Work, who taught me a lot about how families function in the real world.

My colleagues at the Brookings Institution were very supportive of all my endeavors. Although the project was near completion when I joined the staff, my colleagues provided an ideal environment in which to complete it. Special thanks to Judith Light, who suggested the phrase "Timeless Treasures." I am grateful to all my friends who inquired about the book as it progressed through the final stages as often as they encouraged me on my Brookings research project on urban leaders. Special thanks to Mike Armacost, who made it possible for me to join the Brookings staff.

My colleagues on the District of Columbia Financial Control Board, especially Edward Singletary (who read an early draft of the manuscript), Constance Newman, Steve Harlan, Andrew Brimmer, and John Hill, were my cheerleaders throughout. Pat Cooks has been a real treasure in typing successive drafts of this work, which took her evenings and weekends away, but not once did she complain. I want to thank Carol Anderson for her superb copyediting, which clarified my prose and caught the inconsistencies. John Simko at John Wiley deserves special thanks for guiding the manuscript through the complex process to publication. Others who deserve my gratitude include Norlisha Crawford, Brenda Cooper, Tonya Bolden, Sheila Harley, Sidonie Davis, Sharon Harley, Carol Randolph, Regina Drake, Rose Singfield, Dolores Clemmons, Gwen Magee, Marjay Anderson, Ethel Sawyer, Charlayne Hunter-Gault, and members of my support network who commented on various chapters of this book.

Finally, I owe much to the late Alvaro Lopes Martins, who was always there for me.

Of course, all points of view are my own. By sharing my family stories and candid opinions about moral issues, I hope I have given you and your children a useful framework for remembering and discussing your own. *The Ties That Bind* is designed to provoke conversation. If it helps you and your children rediscover the hidden treasure of your heritage, let me know about it. Visit my web site (www.timelessvalues.com). I look forward to hearing from you.

# KEEPING

## THE

## PROMISE

# 1

# Frank Talk About Black Values

To succeed in life, people need a clear inner sense of the right thing to do and the right way to be. No one knew this better than traditional African American families. *The Ties That Bind* represents my rediscovery of their values, standards, and traditions. Their distinctive system of values inspired the best of our past—and now, more important, it offers the truest hope and the surest compass for our children's future. It provides the best answer I know to today's burning question: How can we strengthen our children's souls?

I have spent thirty years as a sociologist thinking about family matters in the context of our rich and opulent black culture and history. For the past twenty or more of those years, I was not always able to distinguish between my scholarly purpose and my practical interest as the mother of a growing son. As a mother, I have shared the deep fears, proud dreams, and intense responsibilities of most parents who have struggled to raise a young person to adulthood in one piece. As a scholar, I have researched the value system that held together the tight-knit black communities that through the ages helped raise Frederick Douglass, Sojourner Truth, and Mary McLeod Bethune down to Martin Luther King Jr., Fannie Lou Hamer, Ella Baker, and countless other moral leaders.

Every black generation, including my own, learned these values in a uniform, crystal-clear fashion. It is therefore up to us to reach back now, celebrate how far we have come, and call out the values again by name so that our children and their children can learn them in a conscientious way.

## A PERSONAL TURNING POINT

I set out to write this book because of a conversation I had one afternoon with a group of friends from the 1960s whom I hadn't seen for years. As we sat around Rose's elegant dining-room table eating her gumbo, we realized that we had a lot to catch up on: marriages, careers, divorces, reconciliations, and especially that most challenging and rewarding part of our lives—children.

Rose and her former husband, Waldorf, had raised their seven children—Cynthia, Lavatryce, Adkins, Alyson, William, Carol, and Ellen—on one of St. Louis's private streets in the West End. They had been fortunate enough to have a bountiful extended family that consisted of two sets of grandparents who were deeply involved with their grandkids. Aunt Eileen, an aunt of Waldorf's, lived with them, and provided baby-sitting and the other help that enabled Rose to hold down a full-time job as an elementary-school teacher. They had brought up their children in the Jack and Jill organization with the other members of St. Louis's black middle class.

Ethel and I met in undergraduate school at Tougaloo College in Mississippi, where we were sisters in the Delta Sigma Theta sorority. A native of Memphis, Tennessee, she became my roommate for a time when we both studied at Washington University's graduate program in sociology. Ethel stayed on in St. Louis after graduate school, and became the dean of a local college. She married and divorced, and is the proud mother of a young adult son, a student.

Inez had been an educator for her entire career. St. Louis was home for her and her husband, a businessman, so she, too, had the advantage of having a large extended family nearby. She beamed as she talked about her two grown daughters, who had finished college. Of the four of us who sat around Rose's table that day, Inez was the only one who was still married.

I had been divorced for about a decade. I left St. Louis in the late 1960s to launch an academic career. My son, Thomas, has been reared mostly in Washington, D.C., with my sister Dorie and her daughter Yodit, who is a year older than Thomas. Dorie and I made our own extended family with each other and an assortment of close friends and their families.

We all had a lot to be grateful for, and we surely counted our blessings. But as we talked, a rising sense of unease crept into our conversation. Despite our good fortune, each of us was worried, and we knew one another too well not to notice. We were old friends who didn't have to explain ourselves to one another.

Here's what was bothering us. Our children had many virtues, but they also had several traits that none of us remembered anyone in our families having in previous generations. In fact, our parents would never have tolerated these traits in their children:

Selfishness

Slothfulness

Materialism

An inability to cope

A fragility of the soul

Where had these traits come from in just one generation? We could not throw up our hands and blame the "times" or "society," no matter how tempting that was, because we knew that one finger pointed out would mean three fingers pointed right back at us. We were the times. We, too, were society. If we accepted responsibility for our parenting, the answer was painful and all too obvious.

Let's face it. In many cases, those of us who achieved middle-class status and beyond moved to the suburbs—to integrated neighborhoods where we sent our children to schools that we considered to be better than those in our old, segregated communities. We moved away from our familiar institutions, hoping that our children would receive and achieve as much as any other American children did. To some degree, we were successful.

Our children have had all the material comforts: music lessons, soccer, tennis, and basketball camps, vacations, phones in their rooms, cars, and so forth. We believed that as young African Americans their dues had been paid by generations before theirs, including our own. We wanted to spare them our own strict upbringing. In short, we gave them a childhood and an adolescence unfettered by serious responsibilities so that they would have more space and freedom to breathe, to dream, and to make a better life than we felt we our-selves had had.

Unfortunately, many of us did not pause to evaluate the implications. No, our children were not abysmal fail-ures. They were not even finished products yet. They were doing well by society's standards. But something important was missing from their lives.

Without any doubt, we were prospering in ways that our Jim Crow–era parents would never have thought possible. Yet despite all that we'd given to our children, we could now see that the gifts our own parents had given us were of far greater worth: Traditional values. Practical dos and don'ts. The shoulds and oughts and musts, as well as the ought nots and should nots that were inculcated in us as toddlers, children, teens, and even as wholesome adults. Traditional African American values.

What went wrong? Where did we lose our way as parents? There is no easy answer. Some of us were too busy marching to the beat of modernity (and post-modernity). Some of us renounced the tried-and-true for the new-and-improved on the say-so of so-called experts. Others had passed on some of what we were taught, but not enough. In hindsight, it was all too easy to see that we were the first generation of African Americans who had failed to pass our traditional values and standards on to their children with the same unifor-mity that our parents did when they entrusted the future to us.

How would our children cope without those values? If they could not get their acts together as adults, what, pray tell, would we reap from our grandchildren? Was there time to teach the old ways to our children, all of whom were already young adults? How were other African American parents and children faring? What would be the fate of millions of poor children growing up in the underclass, where these values, once our daily bread, were now barely in evidence?

These questions and many others that I never voiced to my girlfriends set me on a course of self-examination. This book is the result of that odyssey. It is about rediscovering the traditional values most African Americans of my generation learned from their families at a time when our families were more stable. And it is about why we should and how we could put this value system back into its proper place at the epicenter of our lives.

## BLACK VALUES EXPLAINED

In every previous generation, African Americans, whether parents or not, consciously tried to engender these qualities in their young:

A sense of identity

Faith in God

Respect for others

Honesty and a sense of responsibility

Self-reliance and respect for hard work

Resourcefulness

Belief in education

Resilience

Courage

Integrity

These values molded the character of a people who fought their way out of slavery and the poverty that followed in the rugged years after emancipation. Our grandmothers and grandfathers, and our mothers and fathers, held them dear, used them daily for their very survival, and determinedly taught them to every child in their sphere of influence.

Those early lessons were supposed to remain with young people in a vital way throughout their lives. For me, they are as strong today as they were in the 1940s and 1950s when I was growing up. Without those lessons to draw on, I would have failed many more times than I have. I would not have been able to endure the horrors of segregation and the difficulties I encountered in the civil rights movement, including going to jail. I would not have been able to rise above my working-class background, graduate from high school, and earn a college degree. The values planted by my parents and developed in childhood have seen me through major illnesses and career challenges, and actually gave me more grit and determination to rise above personal difficulties as the years went by.

Four basic principles ran through that value system.

1. **The power of self-identity.** Few groups in American society have had to struggle as long or as hard as African-Americans for their basic humanity. For no other group has the quest for a positive identity been more complex. Thus lessons in black values frequently teach the importance of developing a strong sense of both group and personal identity in the face of conflicting messages about our worth.

2. **The power of the extended family.** Throughout slavery, every effort was made by slaveholders to prevent our ancestors from forming and sustaining families. One could call this period of history the subfamily phase, as did the sociologist Andrew Billingsley, when the slave family was forced to go underground in order to exist

9

at all. Resilience, resistance, self-reliance, and resourcefulness became the dominant tools of the struggle to have a stable family life. Because there is strength in numbers, every member added value to the whole.

3. **The power of the community to determine its future.** Determinedly working together, African American families built communities, churches, and schools. Interdependence was the rule. All of our families wanted the children of the community to succeed, and we wanted our children, when successful, to bear some collective responsibility for those who were less fortunate.

4. **The power of the past to influence the present.** The collective values of black people find their uniqueness in the far-reaching history of slavery. Black values are ultimately centered on the keys to survival. In our traditional communities, we referred to the wise elderly people who taught or embodied those values as "old heads." It was also a term of endearment given to exceptionally insightful young people.

When I was young, I used to love to hear my grandparents, great-aunts and great-uncles, and other elderly people in our neighborhood talk about the old days. They also passed on to us the stories their parents had told them. These stories made me feel a special kinship for my great-grandparents and other ancestors whom I never met. The stories told of how our forebears solved some of the toughest problems any human beings have had to face. I was especially fascinated by the gripping tales of how they outfoxed the people who had done them wrong and coped without losing their dignity. I also remember inspirational stories of their many successes:

buying their own homes and educating their children on the meager salaries they earned as maids, janitors, factory workers, and field hands.

I now realize that my older relatives weren't just spinning yarns. Embodied in these stories of the old days were lessons about character-building, self-esteem, and, in general, ways for us to survive and prosper and become better people. Thus children learned to fight for what they believed was right, to sacrifice to get what they wanted, and, in doing so, to defer gratification. They also learned the importance of patience, having goals, and sacrifice, as well as how to find practical ways to turn dreams into reality.

We looked up to adults because of what they had done and how they had prevailed, not because of what they had. Their values were functional, workable guidelines that applied to everyday life. These values for living involved the most basic elements of survival: the health and welfare of families and children, the viability of neighborhoods, and the building and preservation of churches, schools, lodges, and social institutions. It was through such day-to-day concerns that their ancestors before them had reinforced their sense of authority and purpose as husbands and wives, as parents, sons and daughters, neighbors and friends. It was by successfully fulfilling these roles that they achieved their good names, honor, self-respect, and the respect of others.

I am describing not only my own memories and kin but the common experience of several generations. Black values cut across economic and geographic divisions. While there are some variations in the traditional values of African-Americans who grew up in urban or rural environments—and in the values of those who grew up in poor, working-class, or middle-class families or some combination thereof—these values are essentially the same.

Our ancestors brought some of these values from their old cultures. Others originated during and in response to the Middle Passage and slavery. Still others developed in response to the twentieth century and were severely tested in a national environment of legally recognized segregation. Taken together, they constitute a living legacy.

Our forefathers and mothers kept no special covenant with virtue, and, without question, many failed to live up to the standards they dictated. But they had a talent for setting standards of moral and ethical conduct. Always cunningly creative, they kept these standards intact and used them as they formed families, raised children, expressed their spiritual natures, and generally navigated even more rugged social, political, and economic terrain than we face today.

Some readers are bound to question the wisdom of my writing this book on black values and not on the American values that, as African Americans, we also share. They will wonder whether the differences warrant such a book. To anyone who would argue that values are the color of water, I say that's a fine point of view, as far as it goes. I do not argue with it; I simply add the truth of my observations and cultural experience. Every ethnic group puts its own flavor into the water. For black people, the flavor is rich and deep.

## LOSING OUR WAY

Like most kids, I used to feel that I should have more freedom to make my own rules. Back then, I was annoyed with my parents' "preaching," as I called it behind their backs. "Wait until you get some kids," they would say. "Then you'll appreciate what we're trying to teach you." They were right. As a beneficiary of generations of struggle for survival and advancement, I could not imagine the consequences of materialism, immediate gratification, and lifestyles devoid of self-sacrifice. Our children are paying the price.

Far too many African American children—middle-class, wealthy, and poor alike—do not have a clear set of values to lean on, because we did not give them one. The consequences have been swift and stunning. Many kids do not have a positive sense of their racial or ethnic identity, nor do they know about exemplary, ordinary black heroes and "sheroes" in the past and present. They do not have a sense of belonging to a community of black people that is larger than their immediate families. Our children may have a more comfortable lifestyle than many of us enjoyed when we were young, but they often do not have the strong identity and survival skills they need on the inside, where it really counts.

When middle-class children lack a certain core of values, they experience the kinds of problems my friends and I were discussing over dinner in St. Louis. But when poor children lack those values they are in crisis. They do not have the economic advantages—jobs, incomes, safe homes, and communities that bring stability, if not wisdom—that insulate middle-class children from their confusion or the confusion of others. Most of the black poor are struggling to make ends meet, to abide by the law, and to uphold the values they were taught. But their ability to do so is compromised because their environments are at such high risk, and many are steadily losing ground.

It is easy to become discouraged. Our individual successes notwithstanding, social and economic forces have come together to create an uphill battle for blacks as a group. Since 1960, black families have become so fractured that 48 percent of them are now headed by women. The majority of the children in these families are living in poverty. The infant-mortality rate among blacks continues to increase, as the gap between blacks and whites widens.

The school dropout rate, too, continues to rise. The number of homeless individuals and families, estimated to be as high as 1.2 million, escalates daily. Blacks now make up a disproportionate number of AIDS cases, and have the fastest-growing rate of AIDS of any group in the United States. Teenage pregnancy, though it has slowed, continues to be a problem; many babies have grandparents who are in their mid-twenties. The rates of child abuse and neglect are increasing, especially among drug-addicted mothers and teenage mothers.

Crime and violence have torn many communities apart, undermining stable neighborhoods to such an extent that people now fear for their safety. And drugs have come to symbolize a modern-day plague, both in its seriousness and in its proportions. In Washington, D.C., drug-related violence caused reporters to dub the city "the murder capitol of the nation." I'm talking about young black men in their late teens and early twenties, who were cut down in the prime of their lives, long before they had the opportunity to become husbands, fathers, workers in productive jobs, or socially responsible citizens. More black youths enter prison than enter college each year. A similar pattern has developed among poor, young women, whose prospects are just as bleak. They believe that a bright future with a college degree, a good career, and a good marriage with children is absolutely impossible. They don't value life very much because they don't feel they will live very long.

What can we do? How do we intervene? How do we help these young people to veer off their destructive courses? How do we help to restore a sense of normalcy to our communities so that elderly men and women can walk the streets safely? How do we keep children in school long enough for them to graduate? How do we stop children from having children? The answers to all of these questions require taking this first step: restoring a value system that inspires hope, trust, and a desire to achieve.

Did our failure to endow our children with our value system cause all these problems? Of course not. I do not pretend that restoring a traditional value system alone will solve them. Values, however, are a critical factor. As the old heads used to say, we have to earn our space in this world. Our value system requires us to take responsibility not only for our own successes but for the success of every child among us. Fixing our problems starts with fixing our values.

I have an unshakable faith in our power to heal ourselves. We need to understand that discarding our traditional values is not a precondition for prosperity. To the contrary, living by our values is the precondition. Like every other ethnic American immigrant group, we have to "keep the faith," because we have come so far and aspire to so much. We can participate fully in an integrated society without giving up the essential parts of our culture. We need to teach our children that it is neither necessary nor an option for them—or us—to forsake our heritage of values.

In fact, most of us are already swimming in the mainstream. Our children need to know that. We have failed to communicate this effectively enough. Being black does not mean being poverty-stricken, dejected, or a member of the underclass. It means being culturally distinct because we have unique ties that bind us securely to the past and to the present.

Even though I have explained my intent, some people will be concerned that a book on black values singles African Americans out from the rest of the society and exposes "family secrets" that should be discussed only among ourselves. These same critics will surely ask an important question: Don't these problems and issues also apply to other people?

My answer is yes, they do. As a nation, we are preoccupied with values for a good reason. All of us want to stop the erosion of solid and honorable beliefs and traditions. The lessons in this book can be helpful to anyone who cares about young people. The problems and wisdom of African Americans are certainly not ours alone.

Yet there is a vast difference between what Pat Buchanan means when he says "traditional American values" and what Jesse Jackson means when he says the same thing. In the chapters that follow, I will try to make this distinction clear and lay down a path for our families to travel in order to rediscover and embrace the time-tested values of our heritage.

## YOUR JOURNEY NOW

It is impossible to write a book on values that everyone will agree with. Values are personal. They represent our individual choices and the things we hold to be important. Values, by definition, differ across groups, time, and place. For example, I do not expect all African Americans to agree that the particular values I will discuss in the following chapters are the right ones; other values may loom larger in their memories, and that is to be expected.

This is not a book that seeks to define an absolute code of standards. It is a book that asks you to think about a critical set of questions: What should we teach our children? How can we bring back into the fold those who have lost their way? What was the path of our fathers and mothers that brought us this far? How can we adapt their lessons to our times? This is the quest that I invite you to take with me now, in a journey toward understanding how we can help our children develop clear, functional values.

In the next four chapters of Part One, I offer a closer look at the four fundamental principles underlying the black value system. I show how these principles took root and examine what they mean to us today. In Part Two I share lessons in values from my own Mississippi childhood in order to show how one typical black family passed their values on in a traditional African American context. In Part Three I share my feelings and insights regarding the connection between our values and the two most intimate and vulnerable ties in our lives: our relationships and our children. Finally, in Part Four I give you a number of specific ideas for things you can do now to bring the treasure of the African American value system into your family, church, community, and schools.

# 2

# The First Principle:
## *Identity Determines Personal Power*

In strong, traditional families, children developed a positive self-identity very early in life. In my mother's house, for example, self-esteem was highly valued. However, it was not couched in terms of the word *identity*. Mother simply, frequently, and always quite forcefully said, "Know who you are."

Throughout childhood, all people are engaged to some degree in the often difficult and sometimes tortuous process of sorting out who they are. For our children, race and, in many instances, poverty complicate the process. Unless children have an unshakable basic belief in their worth, the task can easily become overwhelming. Traditional families intuitively understood that.

Erik Erikson, the pioneer of the concept of identity, defines the word as "the creation of a sense of sameness, a unity of personality now felt by the individual and recognized by others as having consistency in time—of being, as it were, an irreversible historical fact." He emphasizes the importance of having both an individual and a group identity if one is to form a mature, healthy personality.

For no other group in American society has the quest for self-identity been more complex than it has been for blacks. Until the 1960s, blacks were portrayed as having a negative self-image, low self-esteem, and general feelings of inadequacy and worthlessness. People like Jackie Robinson, who did not fit the stereotype, were regarded as exceptions to the rule.

The 1960s and early 1970s, however, turned these stereotypes upside down. The civil rights movement had erupted. Young blacks asserted their pride. Deliberate efforts were made to discard negative self-images and labels and to replace them with powerful role models. Independence was equated with being separate and apart from whites. Nationalism flourished as an ideology and as a way of life.

Those who were caught up in the movement placed little value on the development of individual identity during this era. The overwhelming emphasis was placed on developing a healthy racial and ethnic group identity. As the pendulum swings back today, however, we recognize that we need to make room for both our racial and our individual identities.

What does this mean for our children? The child psychiatrists James Comer and Alvin Poussaint sum it up in these words: "All children develop a positive self-image mainly from the consistent love and care of their parents and other significant adults in their environment. This is especially true for the children of minority groups, since parental nurturing must offset the effects of an antagonistic society." As the child's development proceeds, he or she begins to take on other identities. Then, according to Comer, "he identifies with groups—class, race, nation."

## THE POWER OF SELF-IDENTITY

In our traditional communities, it was easier to teach children to know who they were than it is today. Individual identity and group identity went hand in glove. Several factors played a part.

First of all, we were all poor but didn't know it, so to speak, because few of our neighbors had any more than we did. We had enough food to eat and clean clothes to wear; we got a new pair of shoes when the old pair wore out, and we had a roof over our heads. If you had those things, life was pretty good. We didn't expect to have a lot of extras. If someone got a new dress and shoes, it was usually for a specific purpose—a school play, homecoming, Easter Sunday, Christmas, or the Fourth of July.

Second, our lives were bound up in traditions and the expectations that the adults had of us. Most of what we did was meant to affirm their sense of who we were. Our parents put much emphasis on forgoing the materialistic pleasures in the interest of "doing the right thing." We celebrated the smallest things, and we didn't take much for granted: a beautiful sunset, a bountiful harvest, a new baby being born, or a child in the family taking her first step or cutting his first teeth; or being alive, having a family that cared about us, and being secure in the knowledge that if we put forth our best efforts, everything would be all right.

Third, most of our parents had lots of kids, and it seemed that an adult was always close by. I had eight siblings, including Fred, who even as a child showed signs of becoming the very stable man he did indeed become; Willa, a whirlwind from day one; Billie Ruth, Miss Feisty,

Miss Cute, who more than any of us inherited Mother's warm, nurturing ways; Tommy, a born pacifist, with a deep love of animals, and so accident-prone; Archie, an adventurous free spirit; Hazel, the baby of the family, plucky always and forever. Then there was me and Dorie, fifteen months my senior, who would always be the most fearless of us all; and there was Harvey, my oldest brother, who was raised by my maternal grandparents. We were the children of Mother's first marriage.

Ours was a normal existence for a working-class Negro family during those days. My stepfather, Daddy Bill, was a diesel mechanic who was employed by a local General Motors dealership for about twenty years. Although he was a gentle man, he commanded respect and was the undisputed head of our house. Mother almost always deferred to him. "Go ask Bill," I remember her saying whenever there was any doubt or dispute about whether we should do something or go somewhere. "He has the last word in this house." In retrospect, it is easy to see why Daddy Bill was given such pride of place: He was a sensible man and a good provider.

After marrying Daddy Bill, Mother remained a housewife. Daddy Bill did not want her to work as a maid, which was the only type of work that was available to her. "I don't want you to have to toil in some white folks' house like my mother had to do," he told her. "There is enough work for you here at home taking care of the children and this house." And indeed there was. She worked from sunup to sundown, washing, scrubbing, combing hair, mending, cooking. She stretched Daddy Bill's salary farther than one can imagine. And she had an amazing capacity to organize anyone and anything around her. I was assigned the cooking and cleaning chores, while Dorie was the baby-sitter for our younger brothers and sisters. As each child got older, he or she took on some of the responsibilities for the younger children, and more chores, so that each year Mother was able to run the house more efficiently.

We had a steady stream of neighbors coming through our kitchen, where Mother held court, giving advice and providing inspiration. Their conversations wound around to all kinds of things, from children trouble to husband trouble to "female trouble," but Mother always drew the line at gossip.

Mother was also a wonder-worker when it came to the sick. She nursed countless relatives and neighbors back to good health from all sorts of minor and serious ailments. To her children, she also transmitted her strong humanitarian values with almost daily admonitions that we were responsible not only for our own lives but for the lives of others as well. And didn't she practice what she preached!

If Mother saw a neighbor pass our home while drunk, she invited him in for a cup of coffee to sober him up, then gave him a gentle but firm lecture on how he should try to "make something out of your life." Eventually two neighbors, Slangshot and Sa Po, reached the point where they were ashamed or afraid (I'm not sure which) to pass our house.

"Nothing ever goes into a tight fist and nothing ever comes out," Mother frequently intoned. "Everyone has something to give."

Even in the absence of a biological parent, we were taught to love and respect that person. So the distance that separated me from my biological father, Eunice Stafford Ladner, did not prevent me from either acknowledging him as Daddy or from feeling kinship to his lineage. The Ladners were a large Creole family of farmers, artisans, and craftsmen including shipbuilders and cattlemen who amassed more than two thousand acres of land from the Homestead Enactment of

1861–1900 in the areas that now make up the coastal regions of Louisiana and Mississippi. They lived mainly along the Gulf Coast, but operated businesses in such far-flung coastal areas as Florida, Texas, the West Indies, Cuba, and Santo Domingo.

Daddy's father, Grandfather Thomas Fontaine, married my grandmother Della Rose McLeod in southern Mississippi in 1913. Mamma Della and her family had migrated from Georgia to Mississippi when she was a young girl. Following her graduation from Campbell College in Jackson, Mississippi, she married Grandfather Thomas. Their union resulted in five children: Eunice Stafford, my father, who was born in 1914; Charles, Christine, Thomas Fontaine, and Valoise. My grandparents moved to Hattiesburg, Mississippi, in the 1930s and became leaders in the black community. Grandfather Thomas, a well-respected community and church leader at Antioch Baptist Church, was quite literate, and even during a long illness with tuberculosis, he continued to teach literacy and Bible classes to the residents of the community as well as the members of the church.

Like all traditional families, we had family stories that had been nurtured and passed down from one generation to the next. They were stories of fortitude, joy, triumph over adversity, and other critical matters that gave shape to our aspirations and our identity as a unique people who were nonetheless descended from others and linked to generations to come. We were taught that the most important value of all was the self-respect that comes from not bringing dishonor of any kind on ourselves or our family. We were taught to have pride and self-confidence and to be optimistic about our ability "to achieve anything we set our minds to," as my mother would say.

My mother was the great motivator, stressing always that behind every dark cloud is bright sunshine, because she wanted so desperately for us to avoid the pitfalls she had not been able to escape. She was tremendously concerned about our "not failing" and told us often and in many ways that we could and had to succeed. As a result, I knew almost exactly what was acceptable and unacceptable. I craved the approval and acceptance of my family and my neighbors alike, and I clearly understood that good behavior was rewarded and bad behavior was punished.

Finally, segregation, so burdensome for adults, fortified children in many ways. In our churches, schools, and strictly segregated neighborhoods, our African American teachers, preachers, and other caring adults talked often about dignity, carried themselves in a dignified manner, and treated us with respect. A positive group identity therefore developed within the confines of our insular environments. Just as it has been proved that female students in all-girls schools develop a greater capacity for success than do girls in coeducational schools, so did we have greater opportunities for building a positive identity among ourselves in the absence of confusing, inconsistent messages about our abilities. Most African American adults of my generation shared similar early experiences. Everyone did not turn out to be a resounding success; nor were we all raised with the same deeply entrenched values. But, in the main, we knew who we were at a very early age.

## THE CHALLENGE TODAY

Today, most children are still struggling to find themselves. How could that be, despite our love and our efforts? The answer is that their environments are more diverse and diffuse than ours were. There is no "village" or "kitchen" culture to fortify them with coherent, persistent, positive messages that seamlessly affirm their strong identities as good people, valuable individuals, and responsible members of their race.

My son, Thomas, is protected to some extent by the family stories he hears, but family stories are oftentimes lost on children because they receive so many inconsistent messages from the rest of the culture. I cannot protect Thomas in the way that I was protected because my messages to him are constantly competing with more interesting and compelling messages he receives from society and the media—from the sometimes violent, misogynist lyrics of rap music to the violence of the black culture itself. The large number of black men who are embroiled in the criminal justice system or chronically unemployed, and who themselves suffer from broken identities, unwittingly hurt a lot of children, who see themselves when they look into the faces of these young black men who are lost. The same thing happens when girls who are struggling to establish a sense of themselves see other black girls who have been forced or have allowed themselves to be portrayed as ignorant and worthless sex objects.

Today, we also have new ways of relating to our old roles. Women no longer accept the notion that they must remain at home and raise their children, even if they have a choice. With the change in women's options, it is less likely that there will be mothers at home during the day to talk to their children, as might have been in the past. Child care has been turned over to institutions and paid baby-sitters. Husbands and wives who should be active in Parent-Teacher Associations do not have the time to go to meetings anymore. From volunteer activities to cooking the evening meal, our behavior has changed, as harried parents spend less and less time working within their homes and interacting with their communities.

Failure was not an option for me or for many of my peers. Nor should it be an option for our children. Today, however, everyone's weaknesses are passed along. This was not supposed to happen to any of our children. They were all supposed to do better than we did. But identity no longer functions across our culture the way it used to. For some children, identity has broken down completely. And, even among stable families, all but the most involved parents have lost some of the control and, therefore, the influence their parents had.

For better or worse, our children will find their identities as members of our families whether these families are large or small and whether they are isolated from the black community or not. Our circumstances may change, but our children's needs remain essentially the same as ours. They need to feel secure and wanted. They need the healthy sense of self-respect and trust that follows from this knowledge. They need to feel every day that they belong to someone who truly cares about them. And here I am speaking not of belonging to "Mother Africa" in the abstract but of belonging to real, live adult human beings who are constantly present in their lives.

*Traditional values have the power to heal broken and fragile identities. An important purpose of our journey, then, is to discover how each of us can find the will and the means to give more children a positive sense of themselves in this diffuse, diverse, and frequently difficult world.*

# 3

# The Second Principle:
## *We Did Not*
## *Raise Ourselves Alone*

In strong, traditional families, children grew up knowing the names and faces of lots of relatives. Because I was born in the home of my grandparents and grew up surrounded by loving uncles, aunts, and cousins, I took being part of a large, caring clan for granted. Extended families were a fundamental aspect of black culture. A historical tradition imported from Africa, combined with the economic instability that characterized our lives in the New World, had encouraged and strengthened this family structure. In my generation, it influenced every feature of family life—from the teaching of values to the care of babies and old folks. Ironically, though, this was not always the case.

From 1619, when the first slaves landed on American shores, to 1865, when slavery officially ended, the very concept of a slave family was an oxymoron. Our ancestors became chattel property. They were not allowed to speak their own languages or to learn standard English. They could not observe the African religions they had brought with them or practice Christianity except under the watchful eye of their oppressors, who feared that they would use church services to organize rebellions. Most important, they could not legally marry or "own" their children without the possibility of being separated by the commercial demands of the slave trade. At any point, their common-law marriages might be disrupted, because the slaveholders could sell the husband or wife or children without offering the remotest possibility that they would be reunited. Slaves who had built long and durable marriages often suffered the pain of having these relationships destroyed.

Because slavery tried to prevent strong families or, in many cases, any families at all from developing, blacks had to be as creative as possible in forming, defining, and cementing their ties. This was especially critical to the mothers and fathers and children whose fragile human bonds were crushed through separation. In his autobiography, *The Life and Times of Frederick Douglass*, the abolitionist Frederick Douglass plaintively recalls how his own mother, who had been sold to another plantation, slipped into his grandmother's home in the still of the night to see him. Douglass writes: "I was grander upon my mother's knee than a king upon his throne . . . dropped off to sleep, and waked in the morning to find my mother gone. My mother had walked twelve miles to see me, and had the same distance to travel again before the morning sunrise."

Sojourner Truth, the abolitionist, suffragist, and nurse for the Union Army, provides a vivid account of the trauma her mother suffered when she was separated from her children. Sojourner recounts: "I can remember when I was a little, young girl, how my old mammy would sit out of doors in the evenings and look up at the stars and groan, and I would say, 'Mammy, what makes you groan so?' And she would say, 'I am groaning to think of my poor children; they do not know where I be and I don't know where they be. I look up at the stars and they look up at the stars.'"

After emancipation in the rural South, the extended black family sustained the sharecropper economy. However, as more and more families migrated North in search of jobs, a distancing from their extended families began to occur. It was at this point that the stereotypes and myths that blacks don't care about their families were fertilized in the minds of many Americans. Black families were increasingly labeled "matriarchal," "disorganized," "pathological"; and the men were invariably "emasculated" or "violent" and "oppressive."

In reality, while families were greatly challenged by distance and hardship, they continued to gather strength through the embrace of relatives who were nearby as well as those who were "back home," and they reinforced positive values in their children.

## THE POWER OF THE EXTENDED FAMILY

In extended families, children gained an early sense of accountability to many significant others and found plenty of role models who practiced the virtues espoused by the family.

I grew up in a modified compound. On the street behind us, and a few houses over, lived Daddy Bill's parents: Ida Bettis Perryman, whom we called By-Ma, and Bill Perryman, who was known as Paw Paw. We could reach their house by walking along a fence and then through a gate. It was here that Ida and Bill Perryman had raised Daddy Bill, the only child born of their marriage, and Dorothy Jean, a niece of Paw Paw's. And what a character he was. One of his idiosyncrasies was that he painted his car himself—every year, I believe. Fire-engine red. Green. Yellow. And I think he used house paint. Even as an old man, he continued to wear zoot suits, and on one of my visits home in the early seventies I found him wearing platform shoes.

By-Ma was quiet, and so nice to Dorie and me. She gave me a dollar to do my Christmas shopping one year! This dollar had the purchasing power of about $20 today, and with it I bought all of my presents that year, which included a bottle of perfume for By-Ma. "Baby, you didn't have to buy me anything," she said. That's how much the fragrance stank.

Right behind our house, and likewise accessible by a gate, lived Archie Bettis (By-Ma's brother) and his wife, Aunt Icie Bettis. Their house had both a front and a back porch, and consisted of two rooms: a bedroom and a kitchen, the dominant feature of which was one of those fabled potbellied wood stoves. Uncle Archie and Aunt Icie, a childless couple, were very close. And we were among their children.

Aunt Icie and Uncle Archie. Paw Paw and By-Ma. These were just some of the families that were close by. There were more aunts and uncles, and scores of cousins. There were neighbors like Miss Katie and Miss Mary, Miss Florence and Miss Della Galloway, who may as well have been kin, given the roles they played in our young lives.

I would sit underneath the steps of our front porch on hot summer days and listen to Mother, By-Ma, Aunt Icie, and our neighbor, Miss Katie, talk about other people's business. Through these conversations, I began to understand human behavior. I discovered not only the pathos—the sorrow and the pity of being black and poor in rural Mississippi—but the joys and happiness of belonging to a people who were unified and fortified by common bonds of experience, shared goals, and love for one another. I could see that Mother benefited from these conversations, too. She turned to the others for advice on how to raise us children and how to get along with Daddy Bill. And sometimes the older women turned to her for advice, as if they were sisters.

Through good times and bad, family members willingly accepted their mutual dependence. I saw strong evidence of this spirit at work in black families and communities, North and South, East and West, throughout my life. During the summers of my college years, I used to travel to Chicago to work in Spiegel's mail-order house. I was trying to save enough money to help defray my tuition. Each summer, my Uncle Thomas and Aunt Lonnie welcomed me into their home on the South Side because they believed firmly that it was their duty to help their nieces and nephews who were trying to better their economic status. Because of their generosity, born of a tradition of mutual interdependence, I learned the importance of family responsibility firsthand.

When I finished college, I continued the tradition by supporting my younger sisters and brothers through school. What we learned from our benefactors was that it would not be possible to achieve our goals on our own, without the help of others. I would not be where I am today had it not been for the generosity of my aunt and uncle, who made tremendous sacrifices so that I could accomplish my educational goals.

A friend of mine had a life-transforming experience when he received word that one of his five nieces was having trouble back in his hometown of Mississippi. He got into his car and drove for twenty-four hours until he reached their home. Then he returned to Washington, D.C., not only with this niece but with her four sisters as well. He enrolled them in school and sent them to college; one of them is now a physician. It is doubtful that any of his five nieces would have become successful without his kind intervention, but this is what was traditionally meant by "family."

We were expected to help support our younger siblings and cousins. It was only with the older ones helping the younger ones that we could pass on this chain of success. It did not always work smoothly, because, as the saying goes, "people will be people." But the basic principle of mutuality was widely understood and accepted.

## THE CHALLENGE TODAY

Integration began to relieve my generation of some of the burdens of racial responsibility that our elders, "race" men and women, accepted unquestioningly. But as young people, we were still strongly tied to the expectations and rules of our families. Times have changed. Now, there is little social pressure to uphold one's racial group or one's family. Relieved of the burdens of racial responsibility and family expectations, children today are more likely to grow up with little sense of belonging to and being responsible for their racial group and family. The popular notion that they should "go for it" and "get what's theirs" celebrates their individualism to the detriment of their most important group memberships.

When children separate their sense of belonging from their sense of responsibility, we all pay the price. There are children today who expect others—family, neighbors, social-service organizations—to take on the responsibilities that result from their mistakes or misfortunes without making any attempt at reciprocity. Whenever I hear about grandparents being pressed into duty to raise their grandchildren because the parents have abdicated their responsibilities, I know that in that family the old ties have frayed and the tradition of interdependence, though not entirely lost, has been misinterpreted or misunderstood.

But most of us need to give our children opportunities for more interaction with our extended families, not less. I wish my son could have experienced the delights of my childhood—those countless experiences that strengthened my character. If only he could have sat on the back porch with my great-uncle Archie and listened to the Brooklyn Dodgers baseball games. Each time Jackie Robinson came to bat, Uncle Archie's joy was infectious, and we kids would jump and shout with him. We knew those games were about more than baseball: They were about racial pride, courage, and the assurance that we could climb any mountain we set our minds to climb. I wish my nieces and nephews could have eaten Aunt Icie's tea cakes, fresh from the wood stove over which she taught us the importance of sharing.

There were once so many people who cared about each child. Now there are so few. In the next chapter, we will take a close look at several of the key reasons that this is so, including the mobility of modern society.

*When our children have no Aunt Icie and Uncle Archie, it's up to us to find ways to fill the void. Traditional values remind us of the support as well as daily instruction in the art of living that once flowed abundantly in extended families. Another purpose of our journey is to learn how to teach our children the joys and the soul-enriching responsibilities that once automatically stemmed from kinship.*

# 4

# The Third Principle:

## *We Are Making the Future Together*

The third principle underlying our traditional value system is the belief that our destinies are interconnected. To be a member of a community presupposed that one was a part of a close-knit group in which there was a unity of purpose for the common good. Today, many of us ask, "What is the common good?"

The late congressman Adam Clayton Powell had the right idea. "Black people," he said, "must discover a new and creative total involvement with ourselves. We must turn our energies inward toward our homes, our churches, our families, our children, our colleges, our neighborhoods, our businesses, and our communities. Our fraternal and social groups must become an integral part of this creative involvement by using their resources and energy toward constructive fund-raising and community activities. This is no time for cotillions and teas."

I do not claim that people in traditional African American communities were always noble or self-sacrificing. But in days past, more of us understood that it took all of our consistent, collective efforts as a community to help even one child to achieve upward mobility. These efforts were not confined to kin. Most blacks accepted as gospel that their destinies were inextricably bound up with those of the young.

## THE POWER OF THE COMMUNITY

Children in traditional communities discovered sooner or later that their lives mattered to a lot of people whom they barely knew and to whom they were not directly accountable. I remember realizing this when I was in elementary school. On report card day, all the elderly women in my neighborhood would stop me on my way home to inspect my grades. They gave me a dime for every A I made, and they always told me that I was going to be somebody when I grew up. It didn't matter that they themselves probably hadn't finished grade school, or that I was someone else's daughter. They had high hopes for the progress of my generation, and they seemed to live vicariously through our achievements. I never forgot those dimes. To me, they symbolized the faith these women had in me and the strength of their belief in what I could do with my life. They made me feel that I had a responsibility, a duty, to fulfill the expectations of my rural Mississippi community and my race.

Even the less-than-noble forces in the community pushed the young to strive. Palmers Crossing was regarded by most Negroes in southeastern Mississippi as an outlaw community. It acquired this reputation during

World War II, because it was to Palmers that Negro soldiers from nearby Camp Shelby came for entertainment. Since Palmers was outside the Hattiesburg city limits, the sheriff and others who were charged with upholding the law had an easy time looking the other way when it came to the sale of illegal liquor, gambling, and prostitution. There was a price, of course: The sheriff and his deputies received weekly bribes, in cash and "prizes."

Violence was common at the clubs and juke joints. Fights broke out at the slightest provocation. Often, what sparked the fight was only a cover for a deeper anger. Anger at being poor, anger at not having goals or the means to reach those goals, and, above all, anger at the ubiquitous power of white people.

Over and over again, Mother admonished us to steer clear of the juke-joint scene. I used to assure her that her warnings were unnecessary, because I would never want that lifestyle. It held no attraction, no lure, for me. All I saw was women and men with broken and bruised bodies, maimed spirits, and no futures. I wanted a bright future. I wanted to escape Palmers. I knew at a young age that the juke-joint scene promised nothing but entrapment in a life of poverty and misery.

One thing about many of the juke-joint folks that stands out in my mind was their obvious respect for "decent" people. Most of them weren't proud of what they were doing. They did not perceive their behavior as being in any way appropriate or admirable. "It's not the way I was raised...I'm going to get myself straight" was their constant refrain. They were quicker to express shame and contrition over their behavior than is the case today. The tight-knit community of Palmers reinforced a sense of what was right and wrong, so though a lot of rotgut wickedness went on, it never reached epidemic proportions. And the ne'er-do-wells always had an encouraging word for us: "You girls continue to be good little girls and make your mama and daddy proud." If a man had the nerve to make a pass at one of us, these women gave them a tongue-lashing they wouldn't soon forget. "Don't get fresh with this child," they would say. "She's going to be *somebody* when she grows up."

The folks in Palmers Crossing reinforced a strong and clear sense of what was right and what was wrong because that was the only way to insure that the community would survive on its own terms. For example, my teachers were also members of my church, and they did not hesitate to go to my home to report any concern they had about me. This added role of the teachers was acceptable to our parents because they believed in the value of accepting mutual responsibility and cooperation, which is the foundation on which the idea of community is based.

The knowledge that relationships and institutions are connected by the same people, the same beliefs, and the same goals provides a continuity that is nurturing to children. It made me feel that the adults cared about what happened to us. I also felt that they held themselves accountable for how we children turned out.

## THE CHALLENGE TODAY

A highly mobile society like ours, while increasing economic opportunities, contributes greatly to the breakdown and weakening of a community's ties to its children. The average American family can expect to make several moves while its children are growing up. Neighbors change, divorces are frequent, one moves away from relatives, jobs change. The constant movement militates against the development of community. It's impossible to enter into a pact for assuming mutual responsibility for children if you don't know your neighbors or share similar values. Cooperation and a sense of obligation to strangers and kin alike become rarer commodities.

Cooperation and obligation, which are essential to maintaining communities, are also by-products of respect. If authority figures no longer command respect, the resulting turmoil is also likely to undermine the very concept of community. The decline in young people's respect for adults parallels the decline in respect for authority that is so prevalent in today's society. While it is easy to blame individual children for the disrespect they may show adults, I believe that the responsibility must be shared by all the adults in that child's life who have failed to act as responsible role models or, at least, as advocates for virtue in the child. Irresponsible adult attitudes and behavior create a domino effect that works against the community. If adults choose to abandon their roles as models and advocates for good conduct and character, they cannot expect to garner respect or security for themselves.

Other factors have contributed to the erosion of the spirit and fabric of the traditional black community. My generation went off to college in large numbers; some of us met our mates in college and started lives away from our families. In the headlong rush to the suburbs and the misguided beliefs nurtured by the postwar economic boom, many of us thought we could make it on our own, without any help from others. Those who did not, it was said, had only themselves to blame. This assumption was erroneous even then, when government policy sent millions of people, mostly white, to college on the GI Bill and helped even larger numbers to purchase the homes they had dreamed of owning.

To measure how we are doing as communities today,

we need look no further than at our standard for treating our children, our elderly, and our outlaws. Traditional African American communities would have earned high marks for that standard. These communities had little money or power, but they provided everyone, from babies to old folks, with a sense of belonging, identity, and purpose, as well as with food, clothing, and shelter. Outlaws knew their limits and their place.

Today, despite all the good that goes on in our communities, it is no longer uncommon to hear accounts of parents selling their children for drugs, murdering them, or simply abandoning them after birth. The elderly, who are often cared for at home by loving families in the traditional way, also know that it is possible to become the prey of children who at another time in history would have been members of their own extended families.

The boundaries of proper and acceptable behavior continue to expand and push the old rules to the extreme edge. The rewards for good, conforming behavior diminish each day. Even the old adage that crime doesn't pay no longer applies. We've allowed a generation of disruption. There are children who have never developed a sense of right or wrong, of trust and empathy. Desensitized to the trauma of losing even fragile family ties, they care about nothing and no one. Although we are talking about a fairly small percentage of such children, we have to keep the numbers from growing as we make the future together.

*The mood of our communities is primed for reclaiming healing values, traditions, and rules of conduct. While we know that it is not possible to turn the clock back to the days when children could go home after school and be greeted by a mother, a grandmother, an aunt, or an equally caring neighbor, the purpose of our journey is to restore the caring values of our traditional communities for our children today.*

# The Fourth Principle:
## *The Past Is Prologue*

The fourth principle of the traditional black value system is to always remember our unique link to the past. This is very different from romanticizing the past or dwelling on it. We know that it is not possible to stay in the womb. The world has moved forward rapidly, and we must move with it. But the catastrophe of slavery remains an indelible part of our story.

Confusion on this point is a dangerous illusion for the young. It is also common. In truth, it is impossible for any of us, regardless of our age, to conceive of being owned by someone else. Such an idea does not have a vocabulary in modern terms, nor are we truly capable of engendering empathy with our slave ancestors or of getting inside the minds of the slaveholders. Both experiences are outside the realm of probability as we know it. People do not automatically carry living, vital feelings from one generation to the next.

Moreover, we have only recently begun to teach our children the history of slavery. Whereas Jews, for example, said "never again" would they allow another holocaust, blacks said, "Don't remind me." Prior generations rushed to forget the horrors of slavery and the perverse power of racism. Others were all too ready to close their eyes to the past as well, even though the nation itself shares this difficult, tenacious, though potentially redemptive, legacy with us.

Values formed in the cauldron of slavery might have been lost through our amnesia but for one fact: The struggle for black survival never ended, and it continues today in new forms and for both old and new reasons.

## THE POWER OF THE PAST

This is probably the first generation of African American children who have escaped having firsthand knowledge of life under Jim Crow segregation. They must turn to history to learn that for nearly one hundred years after emancipation, racism kept blacks in a state of siege in their own country.

In the America of my generation's youth, blacks had no rights in the workplace. They worked on jobs where quitting time was when the white employer said you could go home. Unions were segregated to exclude black workers, so they worked for whatever amount the employer decided to pay. There were no bargaining rights. In fact, simply asking for more wages might have been considered "arrogant" or "uppity," and one could have been blacklisted for life. My dad's wages were always lower than those of the white men with whom he worked. He never had the privilege of making extra money to put away for the proverbial rainy day. Each and every day was rainy.

Racism was rampant in Mississippi. Segregation stretched its tentacles into every nook and cranny, every crevice, of our lives. Moreover, the consequences of stepping out of line could be fatal. The rules of race were loose and freewheeling. With little or no evidence, the black "guilty" were both defined and judged by their white accusers. In this environment of ongoing hostility, all African Americans had to know the rules for "proper" behavior at all times. Ignorance of even the subtleties of these rules was rarely forgiven; many blacks went to their deaths without knowing the exact nature of the offenses they had been accused of committing.

Still, this was considered progress, for it was a far remove from the agony our forebears had suffered from their backbreaking labor in the fields; from the lashes that came from the leather whips of overseers, or the rapes that countless black women had endured; from being sold away from your children or having them sold away from you. But progress was slow and still required survival-oriented values. No one was confused on that point.

## THE CHALLENGE TODAY

Living in the wake of this turbulent history, it may come as a shock to realize that our children need survival-oriented values as much as we did. My son, Thomas, put it this way: "Mom, you grew up with segregation and you knew what you had to do to fight and get rid of racism. We don't have separate water fountains and rest rooms. We can eat at lunch counters, and we don't have to ride in the back of the bus. But we still have problems, because it works on your mind. The cops will pull my friends and me over just to harass us. They think all young black men are criminals. They try to make you feel inferior just for the heck of it."

Today, subtle and insidious forms of discrimination play, in Thomas's words, "mind games" on our kids, and over time cause them to have a lot of anger. They can't fight the cops who pull them over and frisk them without fear of incurring bodily harm, and possibly death. One night Thomas was out at a party with his friend Jabari. They were stopped on their way home by the cops, put against the wall of a building, and frisked. Then Thomas was given a ticket, but none of the possible offenses had been checked off. Instead, the cop had written across the top of the ticket WARNING.

My question later was: "Warning for what?" Despite a phone call to the police station to inquire, no one could explain why these two boys were being "warned." It was simply an accident of racial harassment, and it was very similar to many such incidents that I had experienced repeatedly as a child growing up in the shadow of racial discrimination.

My parents taught me the skills that I needed to cope with this kind of injustice. But I had not anticipated the need to pass them on to my son. Also, I was fortunate in that I grew up in the midst of the civil rights movement, which affirmed my strong sense of self as a valuable person. Young people today have no such movement or ideology and culture readily available. Yet they, too, need a strong sense of self, as does every generation, if they are to rise to the challenge of the future.

Urbanization, technology, and the changing role of women are good examples of the unprecedented shifts in the larger society that are setting the stage for our children's future. Black families are a part of these global changes. The most fortunate among us, those who are prepared to rise with the tide, have moved securely into the middle class and prospered materially and spiritually with their families and traditional values intact. Strong black families are legion.

As a people, despite our economic problems, we have excelled. In my own family, we have produced our share of social workers, teachers, bankers, and businessmen and -women. More African Americans are going to college and entering careers that were once closed to us, and we are found in virtually all occupations, from Supreme Court justice to astronaut.

Yet many of us remain trapped in a fragile mobility that limits our climb up the economic ladder. Many of us are only a paycheck away from poverty, and most of us have reached middle-class status only by having two paychecks in the family. Two hands were on the bootstrap that pulled us out of poverty, and if one partner gets sick or loses a job we run the risk of a backward slide.

Economic progress does not guarantee us security or wisdom. To the contrary, often economic progress has had this unexpected result: We have abandoned many of our values, but we haven't always known what to replace them with.

Our children are expected to grow and mature in the midst of some very tough and difficult choices and influences. When we adults have gotten ourselves together in terms of what we believe in, and are clear about how we want to live our lives in a purposeful way, it will not be so difficult to prepare our children for the challenges that await them.

*Here, then, is the timeless value system of the elders to help us all survive this era with our children's spirits intact. As the past recedes behind us, we may have abandoned some of these values without knowing what to put in their place. Now we know that we are wise to bring our values with us as we go forward. I treasure these lessons from my traditional childhood. I encourage you to use them to help recall the treasured lessons of your personal past and family history. In calling out the names of our values, each of us is calling back the spirit of our wisest ancestors.*

# THE BLACK VALUE SYSTEM— TIMELESS TIES THAT BIND

# 6

# The First Lesson:

## *Remember Where You Came From*

I remember arriving in Dar es Salaam, the coastal capital of Tanzania, on a hot July night in 1970. My friends Walter and Pat Rodney were waiting for me at the airport by the time I cleared immigration. Walter was a professor of history at the University of Dar es Salaam, and Pat was a nurse at a local clinic. As we embraced, a man walked up to us. He embraced Walter and then Pat, saying to her, "And how is Mama Chaka doing?"

In Tanzania, where identity is traditionally a family affair, it is the custom for a mother to take on the name of her oldest child. The Rodneys' oldest child was a boy named Chaka.

At that instant, despite the fact that this custom was new to me, I was transported in time to my own home-

town of Palmers Crossing, outside Hattiesburg, Mississippi, and the countless times adults had said to me,
"You're Annie Ruth's girl, aren't you?" Annie Ruth was,
of course, my mother. Mother was brown-skinned, with
long wavy hair and Indian features. Daddy Bill often
teased her, calling her an "Indian woman," which she
didn't like. Although she was very friendly, she was a
strong woman whose views were firm, clear, and
straightforward.

Being Annie Ruth's daughter meant several things.
First, it meant that no one "messed with" me because
Annie Ruth didn't allow anyone to mistreat her children.
This was understood whether it was men who might
have gotten "fresh" or other kids who might have called
me out of my name. (To be called out of your name was
similar to what young people today refer to as "dissing,"
or disrespecting you.) Once a neighbor made a pass at
me. I resisted and ran home to tell Mother. She wasted
no time in tracking him down, whereupon she shook her
finger in his face and told him he was never to do it
again. Her words were delivered in such a threatening
way that I knew she would beat this man with her bare
fists if she had to. The man dropped his head and mum-
bled something about his intentions being misunderstood. He was only trying to be friendly, he said. Annie
Ruth was strict with everyone, including us. She wasn't
about to let her children "run loose," as she put it, as if
we didn't "belong to nobody."

Being her daughter meant that I always had to work
harder than anyone else; be cleaner and neater, with my
hair, face, arms, and legs greased down with Vaseline to
avoid being called ashy (that's why I don't like the feel of
grease on my hands today). I had to be more well-spoken
(no Ebonics, or what she called "broken English") and
punctual. My sisters and brothers and I were expected to
be serious and committed to our undertakings—we had

to give 100 percent whenever possible. Because we were black, she preached to us time and again, the odds were stacked against us and we had to work and study twice as hard as white people if we expected to succeed in life.

We heard the same sermons repeated over and over again by our grandparents, great-aunt and great-uncle, aunts and uncles, well-wishing neighbors, teachers, preachers, and anyone who thought we had some potential: We had "no room to slumber." We not only had to work harder and be neat and dignified in appearance but we had to take pride in our work. "If you don't take pride in yourself, who do you think is going to have it for you?" Annie Ruth always said.

Pride and dignity were critically important to her, but knowing who we were was the most important thing of all. In Annie Ruth's words, "It is a sin and a shame for a person to not know where he came from." It was even worse for a person to "forget" where he came from. So she reared us with a strong sense of family history, cultivated almost ritually from generation to generation.

Mother's father, Grandfather Joe Woulard, was the grandson of one Ben Woulard, a white planter businessman, and bounty hunter, and Mary, his Creek Indian mistress. Mary and Ben were born in 1805, in Rockingham County, North Carolina. Along with Ben's parents and his brother, Ben and Mary homesteaded in Washington County, Alabama, in the mid-1820s.

Mary moved to the nearby town of Eret, Mississippi, on the Alabama border, not far from Mobile. There she bore five children by Ben: Frank (b. 1825), Martha (b. 1840), Thomas (b. 1842), Francis (b. 1850), and Jerry (b. 1855). Jerry was the father of nine children, one of whom was my maternal grandfather, Joe Woulard, whom we called Papa. Despite custom, Grandpa Ben did not enslave the five children he had by Grandmama Mary. According to our family oral history, Ben said he "did not want his blood (spilled) all over the country."

Ben also had a white wife, Unity Wiliford, to whom he was legally married. She came from nearby Washington County, Alabama. According to the U.S. Census, they had nine children, and she died when she was in her forties. Again, the oral history passed down by each generation states that whenever Ben wanted to visit Mary in Eret, which was three miles away, he told Unity he was going to have a cup of coffee with a friend. In fact, he traveled to see his lifelong concubine and their five children. It's said that at one point, however, he brought one of those black children to live with him and Unity, possibly as a companion to one of their children.

When I was a child, Mother often told us that Grandpa Ben captured the notorious Copeland gang, which in our minds rivaled the infamous Jesse James gang. She also said that Ben's name and picture were in a "book in the library."

I am a fifth-generation descendant of Ben and Mary Woulard. My older sister, Dorie, discovered this book when she began her genealogical research at the State Archives in Jackson, Mississippi, in 1994. It was there that she found the "book in the library" that became a part of the family legend. This book, *The Confessions of James Copeland*, was dictated by a Dr. Pitts in the 1870s.

Papa was an independent spirit, like his forebears. He was also quite literate, so much so that he handled business affairs for illiterate blacks and whites. He had attended a freedman's school during Reconstruction, and his father, Grandpa Jerry, had been a prosperous farmer. The government tried to get Papa to move West when Native Americans were being forcibly moved to Oklahoma. He refused to go, remained in Mississippi, and married my grandmother, Martha Gates. They had eleven children, the fifth being Annie Ruth.

Papa was an entrepreneur who organized work crews for farm labor, and he also managed a baseball team. He often left Mama and their kids to take the baseball team to nearby towns such as Mobile, Alabama. On one of these trips, as the legend goes, he returned home very excited. "You'll never guess what I spent the night doing," he said to Mama and the kids.

"Tell us about it," Mama said. Papa told them, "I stayed up all night trying to blow out that new lamp they have that hangs from the ceiling. I blew and blew and blew that thing, but it wouldn't go out." Poor Papa. No one told him that he had tried to blow out the very first electric lightbulb he had seen.

Ironically, I would be drawn back to Papa's beloved Mobile in 1996, when Dorie and our white cousins, Sandra Doolittle and her sister Nita Hirsch, discovered each other through their mutual genealogical research. Sandra, who lives in Columbus, Georgia, and Nita, who lives in England, are the fifth-generation descendants of Ben and Unity, just as Dorie and I are fifth-generation granddaughters of Ben and Mary. During two brief reunions, which were attended by Uncle Prince and Uncle Luther as well as by Sandra and Nita's eighty-year-old Aunt Louise, we went back to the homestead and to Mt. Nebo Baptist Church, which Grandmother Mary and her descendants had attended for well over one hundred years. We each shared family legends, filling in the gaps for one another. These legends were passed on from Grandpa Ben and Grandma Mary to Papa's father, Papa, and on to his eleven children. Grandpa Ben's story was repeated often by Mother as well as by her brothers Luther, Joe, Jerry (J.P.), Prince, Arthur Neal, and Lon, and her sisters Oneta, Mary, LeDrester, and Lucy Mae. I see their strong family identity as instrumental in making them the spirited, passionate, and independent-minded people they are.

They brought their forebears' spirit, passion, and independence to just about anything that was important to them. None of my uncles ever had long-term jobs in which they worked for someone else. Each managed to work for himself—as the owner of a small business—and most of my aunts did the same. Mother stopped working—at an ammunition factory and as a maid during World War II—after I was born.

With the slightest provocation, my uncles would break into one of their "Papa stories" and create such vivid visual imagery of him that I felt I was watching my grandfather engaged in animated conversation with the contract laborers whom he hired out to whites; navigating the sophisticated city of Mobile with the baseball team he managed; and, most of all, giving advice and counsel to his neighbors from far and wide who sought him out for his wisdom. He was educated, "good with figures," they say, and carried himself upright with a strong sense of pride and self-respect. Papa, according to my uncles and aunts, was always in charge, and Mama (my grandmother Martha) was his very strong and loyal helpmate.

My coming-of-age in Mississippi was negotiated successfully because Annie Ruth, as well as all of her helpers—aunts and uncles, grandparents, teachers, neighbors, and others—taught us how to see the world from the perspective of Mary and Ben. Through the example of their care and support of their five children, this complex relationship bore the marks of love and commitment that shaped their descendants' identity.

Most African Americans have a mixed racial ancestry, and it is often as complicated as mine. I am reminded of W. E. B. Du Bois' idea of "double consciousness," in which "one ever feels his twoness—an American and a Negro; two souls, two thoughts, two unreconciled strivings, two warring ideals in one dark body whose

58

dogged strength alone keeps it from being torn asunder." The "twoness" Du Bois refers to describes the feelings of a majority of blacks who find the influence of mainstream culture inescapable. It is strongly reflected in many African Americans' ambivalence toward their culture. Some live day to day with the tensions of this "double consciousness," of trying to fit into both worlds.

The dogged strength to which Du Bois refers is the drive that allows one to reach deep inside oneself and find the strength to convert those tensions into energy and will.

Mother had no wholesale abhorrence of white people. She never said, for example, that all white people are evil. She always reminded us that "all people are equal in the eyes of God," and taught us to try to "see the good in everyone," as she would say, "even white people who don't treat the colored people right." Of course, Mother couldn't always practice what she preached. Nevertheless, she did try to keep us above hatred of white people, knowing that if it took root, it would surely warp our souls.

Mother's tolerance of white people had a lot to do with the fact that she had a fairly close relationship with a number of them. For at least twenty years, she had a friendship with a clerk at Hudson's furniture store, a Miss Heddie, who was about Mother's age. I think their friendship began when Mother started preparing hot lunches for some of the white women at the store, one of the ways in which she made extra money. Of this group of three or four women, Mother and Miss Heddie became good friends—to the point where Mother's lunches were exchanged for a sofa, an easy chair, and, once, a lovely dining-room set. We children used to tease Mother about how she worked Miss Heddie, as we watched her cook a midday meal of smothered chicken, rice and gravy, collard greens, candied sweet potatoes, corn bread, and her special peach cobbler. "After you fatten Miss Heddie up with this good food," we teased, "bet you come home with a new bedroom suite." Mother would blush and say, "I can't help it if Miss Heddie likes my peach cobbler that much." Mother, we kids agreed, was a survivor. And she survived with such a deft touch, without compromising her dignity, without bowing her head one bit, as she reminded us repeatedly.

As for what prompted Miss Heddie's lavish exchanges, it may very well have been motivated by sheer fondness for Mother and her good cooking, though I strongly suspect that she was also getting back at H. C. Hudson, who owned the store, for paying her such low wages. During one of my trips home when I was long grown, I asked Mother, "What ever happened to Miss Heddie?"

"Oh, you know, she died a few years ago," she replied. After a moment of reminiscence, she added, "She was a nice woman. Being white didn't faze her at all."

"What do you mean?" I asked.

"Well, you see, she could come here and sit down at my kitchen table and eat and talk like she was colored. Child, me and Miss Heddie used to laugh about the same things. I didn't bit more notice that she was a white woman. She was just like any other human being."

Mother's attitudes about race were undoubtedly a result of her childhood experiences, and her ancestry. As I've mentioned, when we teased Mother about Miss Heddie she "blushed"; and she had long black wavy hair. On their birth certificates, Mother and her ten siblings were categorized as "mulatto." In actuality, they were part Negro, part white, and a mixture of Choctaw and Creek Indian.

"How can you be a mulatto in Mississippi?" I once asked Mother.

"Because that's what we were," she said quietly but

firmly. "We were colored. That didn't mean we thought we were white."

Mother had grown up in an atypical Mississippi community. In the cocoon of Battles everyone was poor, and Mother remembered that the coloreds and the whites were mutually dependent, helping one another through the harsh economic crises. It was a place where race was less important than survival. Poverty was not the only bond. Bloodlines had already been crossed in a thousand ways, and everyone knew everybody else's ancestry. Very few people could honestly claim to be pure anything. That's why Mother simply stated a truism in answer to what I thought was a very complex question: How can you be a mulatto in Mississippi? Because she was one.

Prior to my asking her about her racial status, I don't think she had ever given it much thought. All she knew was that she never believed she was less than whites, and in this regard her father, Joseph Woulard, grandson of a white man, was her first role model. Papa had always perceived himself to be "as good as any white person." To avoid being treated otherwise, he kept himself as independent of white people as possible. He managed this by never working for anyone but himself. Known as Cap'n Joe to everybody in Wayne County (where Waynesboro and Battles are located), he was for most of his life a labor contractor, organizing and managing Negro crews to do construction work, cut and haul timber, lay railway tires, and similar work. He worked hard and true and was held in high esteem. "When I was a little boy," Uncle J.P. once recalled, "I used to hear whites and Negroes declare, 'If Cap'n Joe said it, then that's it.' Those Negro men would follow him anywhere to work. He was sought out by Negroes and whites alike for his advice because he was trusted and respected." Papa's children remembered, too, that he always voted, at a time when masses of Negroes were terrorized out of exercising this right, and he was the only Negro who served as a juror in the county from the turn of the century through the Depression.

"Always get yourselves in a position to work for yourself so you don't have to take orders from anybody," Papa told his children time and again. In their early years, the Woulard boys, six in all, were pulpwood haulers, and later most of them worked as independent contractors. They were paid for the number of truckloads of pulpwood that they cut and delivered to the sawmill, and they believed it was their birthright to be paid the same amount their white counterparts were paid. This is why on one occasion, in the 1940s, when Uncle J.P. learned that a sawmill in Hattiesburg was paying the white contractors more than they paid him, he pulled a strike. "I had all the men who were working for me load their trucks and take them to the mill," Uncle J.P. recalled with a chuckle. "Then we refused to unload the wood. We just sat down. They had to shut down the plant and negotiate with me."

The Woulard boys eventually went into other lines of work, but always they were their own bosses—small stores and restaurants, and as independent plumbers, carpenters, and electricians. Papa's doctrines weren't lost on his girl children, either. Aunt LeDrester, for instance, had a little business as a seamstress. During a period when she worked as a maid, she did so entirely on her own terms. She'd advise the Miss Anne of the hours that she was willing to work, the pay she expected, and the fact that she would have to bring her twin grandchildren, for whom she baby-sat. If Aunt LeDrester's employer couldn't meet her requirements, she refused to work for her. I often teased her about how she controlled the white women she purported to work for. She'd laugh and say, "If she wants me to work, then she's got to work on my terms. I really couldn't care one way or another what she thinks." Aunt LeDrester had a large clientele for her services as a seamstress. She did the maid work only on the side.

And so, the Woulard children passed their father's legacy on to the next generation.

"If you get rid of your pride," I can still hear Mother saying, "you don't have anything left."

And all the while white society was telling me that I and mine were nothing, every day, in all things great and small. Thankfully, there was my family and the family stories of strength and courage that had been passed down, to counter this white madness.

I came from a family of survivors. Each generation of our family has taught the next that we could transcend every obstacle and ultimately prevail. In Mother's words, we had only to "put our minds to it," and "work hard." "Know who you are," but learn how to turn this self-acceptance into a meaningful way to take care of yourself and make a living. Mother felt duty-bound to pass the family history on to us. She emphasized that God made all of us, and we should be proud of our ancestry, including our class. "After all," she said, "all the other black people we know came from similar places."

Knowing myself meant having my feet planted firmly on the ground—knowing where I was going, but never forgetting where I had come from, and being proud of it. Keeping these strictures in mind, I was obliged to earn and protect my good name, my good reputation, for my own sake and that of our family. My parents made it very clear to us kids that we could not bring dishonor to or in any way tarnish the good name of our family. We had to be the very best we were capable of being, stay away from scandal and disreputable people, and carry the family name forward in a positive way.

"If you lie down with dogs you'll get up with fleas" was another of Annie Ruth's sayings. As a child, I didn't understand fully what this meant, but I knew it was important. As an adult, I understand that the reason my elders put such strong emphasis on protecting our name was that they didn't have anything to trade on except the family name. They had no wealth, prestige, education, or high social status that could command respect from others. Their most precious asset was a solid, respectable family reputation. For Annie Ruth, a good name was more important than "all the riches in the world." When she sermonized about the virtues of respect and reputation, she told us that the blacks in our community who owned nightclubs and juke joints had money, but they did not have the respect of their neighbors, nor did they have good reputations. That is why my parents were so concerned that we not play loose and dangerous with our conduct. They knew that if any of us lost the sense of who we were, what our goals were, and where we expected to go in life (and possibly how to get there), we really would have little else left.

Annie Ruth listened carefully to the stories of the old heads that embodied the virtues, and she taught them to my brothers, my sisters, and me. We did not have to reach back to Africa to find our sense of pride. My parents would not have known much about Africa, certainly not enough to choose African names for their children. But they did know and respect their own relatives, especially the ones who were close, and they felt that it was important to pass those names on to us. Hence my middle name, which I share with my older sister, Dorie, is Ann, short for Annie—Mother's first name.

All my sisters and brothers were named for members of the family. I, in turn, named my son for my deceased younger brother Tommy. It is a name that is shared, as well, with my paternal grandfather, Thomas Ladner, and his son Thomas. That is how our parents passed on the family's history and connected the links between us and the generations before us. This tradition made family real, tangible, and our identities as family members crystal-clear and perceptible. Our own relatives were the heroes and "sheroes" of our past, who gave our parents the will to inspire in their own children the virtues of pride, dignity, and self-respect.

Yet I recognize that our view of the world is wider than it used to be. For example, I have nieces named Yodit, Ayanna, and Kanini, and a nephew named Kojo. Yodit, who is my sister Dorie's daughter, is Ethiopian American. I named Kanini for Walter and Pat Rodney's daughter. Kojo and Ayanna are names my sisters and their husbands gave to their children. Annie Ruth also recognized that times change, for she learned to pronounce their names as easily as she pronounced those of her grandchildren who had traditional names: Randy, Tanya, Pamela, Tommy, Charlene, Frederick, Thomas, and Misty.

These are the thoughts that washed over me as I stood in the airport in Tanzania. "Knowing who you are and not forgetting where you came from" echoed in my head with voices that spoke to me from as far back in my own family as I can remember. In transposing the Tanzanian culture to my family, Mother becomes Mama Harvey, after my oldest brother; and I am Mama Thomas, after my only child.

I have come to understand that "Mama Chaka" really meant that Pat Rodney, as a mother, would mold her son and her other children in the same way that her parents had molded her. In this way, too, had Annie Ruth molded me, and I, in turn, have endeavored to leave my imprint on my son, Thomas. In that way, I have earned the right to be called Mama Thomas.

This is the promise. This is the future.

*"Knowing where you came from" means valuing your forebears and living according to the virtues they taught you. Life brings countless opportunities to carry oneself the right way, countless chances to practice the virtues of respect, honesty, integrity, and responsibility you were taught as a child. At any given time during this sojourn, there are temptations that can pull you off course if you let them. But you are honor-bound to improve your family's lot, not to lower it.*

# 7

# The Second Lesson:

## *Trust in the Lord*

Sojourner Truth once said, "I have borne thirteen children and seen most of 'em sold into slavery and when I cried out with my mother's grief, none but Jesus helped me." Born Isabella Baumfree in upstate New York, she later took the name Sojourner Truth because she said she was destined to travel the nation spreading the gospel of freedom.

She would have understood the old Negro spiritual that goes like this:

> *I will trust in the Lord, Oh I will trust in the Lord,*
> *I will trust in the Lord till I die, till I die,*
> *I will trust in the Lord, I will trust in the Lord,*
> *I will trust in the Lord, till I die.*

Trust in God was simple for our ancestors. Faith—a belief in the certitude of God as a higher power who would watch over them—was a necessity. They had to find a way to explain why they were consigned to endure such hardships. They had to believe in and trust that God or Jesus Christ, the son of God, would be there to guide and take care of them; to steer them away from as much "hurt, harm, and danger as possible until the 'sweeter by-and-by,'" as the Reverend Smith, one of my childhood preachers, used to say.

Everyone had a church home. Everyone belonged to a church. Church membership went back generations. Mt. Nebo Baptist Church was founded by my maternal ancestors more than a century and a half ago. When I was a little girl, Mother used to take all of us kids "over home," as she called it, to homecoming at Mt. Nebo—back to the little village of Battles, on the site of Woulard's Bend, the place of my birth. Relatives came from Michigan and Illinois, Ohio, Florida, as well as Hattiesburg and Columbia, Mississippi, to go to Mt. Nebo. Homecoming was always held on the fourth Sunday in September, and no matter what you were doing, or what your obligations were, you always tried to clear the slate so you could get back to Mt. Nebo for the spiritual nourishment in the church; to tend to the ancestral grave sites in the graveyard behind the church; to eat the good home-cooked food in the "dinner on the grounds"—always lots of fried chicken, potato salad, pound cakes, jelly cakes, coconut cakes, sweet potato pies, and lemonade—and just about anything else your heart desired. We kids ate so much that our stomachs always hurt afterward. "Stop gorging yourself or you're going to get a bellyache," Mother warned. "Then you're going to be sick all the way home." Despite her threats, we kids (and some adults, too) ate and ate.

And there were cousins, cousins, cousins, as well as

my grandma Martha, my step-grandfather Ben "Bud" Battles, and many of my six uncles and five aunts. What I remember most is how we kids used to sit quietly in church, with "nary a whisper," as Mother rolled her eyes at us. There was not a word from us until we got outside to eat, play, and get to know our cousins and other relatives, some of whom we were meeting for the first time. I felt the joy and jubilation of celebrating the old ways, and the security of knowing that I had a family. I was merely a speck in the life of this large family, but I never doubted that I was an important speck.

On the drive back to Hattiesburg, which took about three hours, Mother was always animated, joyous that she had been "with family over home."

"Bill, did you see Coun' Doak?" she asked Daddy Bill. "You know, she was the one who was wearing the black hat," she tried unsuccessfully to explain.

For the most part, he didn't have the slightest clue. He was an anomaly—an only child among black folks who usually had at least eight or nine children. This infectious laughter and "big arms wrapped around all these cousins" was not something that he was used to. But he tolerated it well, and seemed to enjoy standing on the sidelines watching Mother revel in the company of her very big family.

Mother was suspicious of the cousins who came to homecoming from "up North," as we called it. "I'll bet they don't have much more than the clothes on their backs," she said. "They come home dressed to kill, but they say life is real hard up North." Daddy Bill was always very quiet. He usually drove silently as Mother talked. Occasionally, he would chime in, or Dorie, Fred, Willa, or I would say something.

"Mother, they might live real good up North," I said once.

"Now you be quiet 'cause you don't know what

you're talking about," she said as she gave me a side-glance from the front seat of the car where she sat. "You're not going to get me way up there to be forgotten by all my kinfolks. At least down here I've got my family. I know where our next meal is coming from—and I've got Mama and Coun' Bud, and Mt. Nebo." Then she'd throw in the names of her sisters and brothers, and I quickly got the picture. Mt. Nebo was not an incidental event in our lives. For Mother, it was a necessity that she would have had to invent had it not already existed.

Their belief in God was a necessity. I cannot imagine how they would have coped without a strong faith that promised them a hereafter and the hope of a better life to come. At the center of our religious belief was the understanding that we had an obligation to be benevolent to the needy. My family taught us that this extended to the dead. Aunt Icie, for example, was a committed mourner. She went to practically every funeral in Palmers and the surrounding territory. The few times she couldn't make it to one, she usually sent me. When I got home, she would want a blow-by-blow account of who was there, who cried, what the dead and the bereaved were wearing, and what the preacher said. She would frequently interrupt me for more details, as well as for her commentary on what I reported.

"They know she didn't look good in pink. Why didn't they put a blue dress on her?"

"It couldn't have been fifty people there, 'cause he didn't know no fifty people."

"He got some nerve whooping and hollering over her in that coffin. He sure didn't cry when she was laying up there sick all those months. God's making him feel guilty, that's all that's about. He scared she gonna come back and haunt him if she ain't already."

"Did he look natural?"

"Tom, we've got to go to that funeral today," I remember Aunt Icie calling out one morning from her back porch across to ours. "That man who lives up on the hill is going to be buried at Priest Creek this evening. He ain't go no kinfolk, so we got to be there so we can be his family." Aunt Icie had nicknamed me Tom because I bore a striking resemblance to my paternal grandfather.

It was a sweltering midsummer Sunday. As always and, like most of her neighbors, she'd gotten up early to cook breakfast and then dinner before the heat got hold of the day. She made biscuits, grits, eggs and beef brains, salt meat, and shrimp with garlic (Creole style) in her old-fashioned potbellied stove. After she finished making breakfast, she would cook her Sunday dinner. That was the meal we children always hoped to be able to eat with her and Uncle Archie.

"Yes, ma'am," I hollered back. "I'll be ready when it's time to go."

We arrived at the funeral early, marched up to the front pew, and sat down. A handful of other church members were there, mostly older women. Though they sat in the back, as if to make it clear that they were no kin to the dead man, still they had come. Even if the man had been drunk almost every day God sent, they thought he deserved a farewell and some remembrance. No one knew where he had come from, or anything about his family, so there was no one to notify when he died. This man had just drifted into Palmers Crossing one day, rented a room in an old lady's house, and did odd jobs between his drinking binges. The people of Palmers looked out for him. Someone would take him by the hand and lead him home if he was too drunk to find his way. He didn't seem to mind, as he staggered up the blacktop hill, oblivious to much else except the brief respite from whatever pain had driven him to the bottle.

Aunt Icie was a true believer that everyone should have a proper funeral, with some family in attendance;

and she was as serious about attending the funerals of those she knew only slightly as she was about attending the funerals of those she knew well. "It's a sin and a shame for that poor man to die and don't even have no family to go to his funeral," she'd say. So if someone didn't have any or much family, she took me by the hand and led me up to the front of the church to stand in for kin and kinfolk who cried and felt all the pain the real family would have felt if they had been there. And throughout this man's funeral Aunt Icie kept repeating, "This po' man is somebody's child. Yes, Lord! Somebody's child."

Thirty years later, I heard these same words after I happened upon a black man lying on the sidewalk near my apartment on New York's Upper East Side. When I ran into a travel agency to ask if I could use the phone to call an ambulance, the personnel refused. They had sat there looking out the plate-glass window at the man for I don't know how long before I found him. And now they flat-out refused to let me call for help. I left and scurried around until I found a pay phone, while an elderly black woman stood watch over the man. When I returned from using the phone, she insisted on waiting with me. "That white woman I work for can wait," said this lady, who was obviously on her way to a job as a domestic. "She ain't going nowhere." As we stood waiting, for about forty minutes, she kept saying, "He is somebody's child."

Two police officers came along, walking their beat, at about the same time the ambulance arrived. They searched the man's pockets and found a rubber tourniquet, so they figured out that he was an addict. They jerked him up off the ground and told him to get moving, and that he shouldn't let them catch him in that neighborhood again. Apparently, he had just been released from a hospital, because he still had on the plastic bracelet. I thought about Aunt Icie when the old lady kept repeating, "He is somebody's child," and I thought about how this black man was the kind of person whose funeral Aunt Icie and I would have attended, sitting right in the front row.

Black Christianity was an activist religion, one that emphasized being "doers," "movers," and "shakers" for social change. Because the religion of black people has never been confined solely to the sacred arena, it has helped to mold our value system since the slaves first sang such spirituals as "Go Down Moses" as a code for the overthrow of slavery.

> *Go down, Moses.*
> *Way down to Egypt land*
> *Tell ole Pharaoh*
> *To let my people go.*

Our slave ancestors adopted Christianity, and accepted as a fundamental tenet that their God would not only grant the believers everlasting life, but would also overthrow slavery and segregation in due time. This was best expressed in the words of another spiritual:

> *Swing low, Sweet chariot,*
> *Coming for to carry me home,*
> *Swing low, Sweet chariot,*
> *Coming for to carry me home.*
>
> *I looked over Jordan*
> *And what did I see*
> *Coming for to carry me home,*
>
> *A band of angels coming after me,*
> *Coming for to carry me home.*

Home was heaven, and God sent the angels for deliverance from the evils of slavery.

Thus God was always seen as an activist who was no respecter of persons but felt that all of us were his children in an equal way. When the time was right, black people began to use their churches to rise up in opposition to destroy segregation and racial discrimination. But the faith of our mothers and fathers was applied to everyday life for the simple and complex purposes of surviving. Communities of sisters and brothers came together to find ways to cope with the tremendous demands that slavery made on them. Faith was necessary in a land that made survival extremely difficult.

As slaves, blacks were powerless to put their traditional African values into practice and greatly restricted as they tried to establish new values in the so-called New World. But they knew that the ability to apply and enforce their own values based on faith was all that stood between the survival or destruction of their embattled communities. And so they found ways to formulate and transfer their own values and community standards. After the Civil War, they began to take their destinies into their own hands and to impose a new social order. They eagerly began reconstructing their lives, establishing themselves within existing communities or establishing their own, and developing a functional code of conduct under the changed circumstances.

Black Americans, as newly recognized citizens of a nation torn by internal warfare, clung tenaciously to one another for emotional, social, economic, and political support. Each individual realized that his or her fate remained linked to the fate of every other member in the community. An abiding faith in God, humility, compassion, and a willingness to forgive were other essential ingredients in the mix of values. These were the values that had helped our ancestors fight their way out of slavery and the material poverty that followed in the wake of emancipation and the ensuing period of Jim Crow and second-class citizenship.

The religious beliefs of the black church have served not only an important secular purpose but a sacred one as well. The most enduring of all the traditional values held by black families across time was an unwavering belief in God. During slavery, Christianity served to help our ancestors cope with oppression, because it promised a life in the hereafter. There, they would be free from the pain, torture, and inhumanity of their lives on earth. Christianity helped make sense of their oppression, and their suffering became more bearable with the promise that they would one day enter "God's kingdom" and enjoy everlasting life. Most important, this promise of a hereafter reinforced a strong belief that justice would prevail and all the wrongs committed against them would be made right. It also taught them patience, fortitude, and the value of delayed gratification, for without these virtues they would surely have surrendered. One might also say that it kept them subservient to their masters in the world, encouraging them to dream of justice in the sky and in the by-and-by instead of the here and now.

The church was the absolute moral authority. Biblical injunctions such as the Ten Commandments were handed down, and we were taught them as law.

1. Thou shalt have no other gods before me.

2. Thou shalt not make unto thee any graven image, or any likeness of any thing that is in heaven above, or that is in the earth beneath, or that is in the water under the earth.

3. Thou shalt not take the name of the LORD thy God in vain; for the LORD will not hold him guiltless that taketh his name in vain.

4. Remember the sabbath day, to keep it holy.

5. Honour thy father and thy mother: that thy days may be long upon the land which the LORD thy God giveth thee.

6. Thou shalt not kill.

7. Thou shalt not commit adultery.

8. Thou shalt not steal.

9. Thou shalt not bear false witness against thy neighbour.

10. Thou shalt not covet thy neighbor's house, thou shalt not covet thy neighbour's wife, nor his manservant, nor his maidservant, nor his ox, nor his ass, nor any thing that is thy neighbour's.

The church, therefore, was also the source of ethics and values that guided our conduct beyond the religious sphere. The church taught compassion, love, mercy, justice, loyalty, responsibility, courage, humility, forgiveness, and tolerance. These virtues were interwoven throughout the fabric of the church organization, encouraging extensive social-welfare activities that included helping the hungry, the homeless, the sick, the orphaned, and the elderly.

The practice of "informal adoption" of children, for example, was promoted by the church, and it came into being following slavery, when families felt that it was their obligation to give a permanent home to children whose parents, for whatever reason, couldn't provide for them. Orphaned children were considered "gift children" in the Negro folk culture of the South, and they had a special place in the hearts of the rural folks. People felt a sense of pity for such a child, and they did everything they could to compensate for the child's loss of parents.

After all, carrying out these Christian duties were considered part of the Lord's plan.

Orphans today are not simply taken in by families, friends, and neighbors as much as they used to be, even though we still practice formal and informal adoption. Orphans' faces now peer out at us from posters and television advertisements urging us to adopt them.

These biblical values were passed down through the generations, and served as a kind of incubator for the civil rights movement. In the 1960s, families took the civil rights cause to their churches because the church was the most independent institution in the community. Black people built their churches with their own resources, and they hired their own ministers; they didn't use any tax money, nor did they solicit donations from white people for their upkeep. Blacks took pride in the ownership of their church—it was theirs and was not subject to scrutiny by anyone for any reason.

When the civil rights movement started in the South, it was to the churches that leaders of the movement turned for a place to meet and for a safe haven. The black minister was one of the few unconstrained people in the community who could take up the mantle of leadership in tough times. Ministers not only led their flocks in matters of religion but they also provided leadership in other vital areas that affected the community. In this sense, the sacred and the secular merged.

Thus religious beliefs and values were infused in the civil rights movement. The minister could preach to his congregation, "Segregation is evil. Therefore God doesn't like segregation, because it is un-Godly." In the face of such evil, religion offered a context, a paradigm of faith, a method of explanation, and a balm for the weary souls of those who came to the church in search of solace. It had steeled their forefathers against greater evil, and it was expected to do as much for them.

Martin Luther King Jr., more than any other black minister in modern times, used religion and the church to advance the civil and human-rights agendas. He organized ministers and their parishioners; he used the churches as a gathering place for meetings; he fashioned a theology, which was articulated in his sermons, speeches, and writings, that used traditional religious values founded in the black church to advance the cause of civil rights.

Today, the church's influence in the secular world has declined. A new generation of African American children and adults are, oftentimes, unaware of the important role the church has played. The traditional role of the church as the voice of moral authority has been weakened. However, we can take a lesson from the many new-breed ministers who are stepping up to the plate to assume responsibility for ministering to the young, teaching them values and giving them a spiritual alternative to our materialistic society.

*"Trusting in the Lord" means helping young people to sustain hope and faith that they can have a future. Lift them up through whatever means you have, and spread the word that they do not have to be hapless victims of self-inflicted destruction or remain victimized by others. Remember the wisdom of the apostle Paul: "Faith is the substance of things hoped for, the evidence of things not seen."*

# 8

# The Third Lesson:

## *Respect Is a Two-Way Street*

Going away to college, I felt truly liberated for the first time. I had long dreamed of the day when I could "be my own boss." The very idea of not having someone to tell me when to come and go, what to do, and with whom to be friendly, I thought, would be something akin to nirvana. I learned quickly, to the contrary, that all the old rules Mother and Daddy Bill had taught me still applied. In fact, the freedom I gained brought a far greater need for rules than I had known at home.

As freshman women, we learned quickly that some of the upper-class guys were literally waiting to pick up spare girlfriends to date on the side. Although they usually had girlfriends with whom they were going steady, or were even engaged, these men wanted to date other women as well. We then had to decide if we were going to begin the apprenticeship program of becoming the "other woman," perhaps establishing a pattern that might have continued beyond college. A few of my classmates did choose to become the other woman, but most of them did not. Those of us who did not insisted instead on being either the only girlfriend or no girlfriend at all, because we remembered our parents' teachings: "If you don't respect yourself, no one else will."

Self-respect is a prerequisite for gaining the respect of others. Feeling self-respect, even as a young person, helped me to define who I was, individually and as a member of my family and the community. The desire to have the respect of others made me act in ways that marked me as someone who took special care to protect, cultivate, and nurture positive and honest relationships with family, friends, and the community. The decision not to become the other woman in a man's life was an example of choosing to maximize my own worth and value. I learned early that it is not possible to have self-respect unless you have tried to put your best foot forward as often as possible. To agree to be second best in any area over which you had control was unacceptable.

Your reputation was closely tied to the amount of respect you commanded from others. My mother often said to us, "Folks are going to treat you the way you act. If you act decent, you'll be treated decent. If you act like a tramp, you'll be treated like one." The desire to protect their reputation kept African American men and women within the community's boundaries of acceptable behavior. Here, again, my mother's words echo: "You can spend a whole life building a good reputation and lose it in a split second if you aren't careful."

Why was there such emphasis on respect, particularly in the sense of its connection to respectability, in traditional communities? Why were youths repeatedly counseled to go to such great lengths to earn and keep good names among their elders and peers? This is a recurring theme in the black value system: While money and material comforts were not readily accessible, recognition as a respectable and honorable person was not only available but was considered a worthy reward. In small communities where neighbors knew one another well, upholding one's good name became very important. Adherence to traditional values meant attempting to avoid dishonor at all costs.

The fact that respect was so important in traditional African American society made the converse, shame, perhaps the most potent means of reinforcing the rules of proper conduct. If, for example, a boy got a girl pregnant, he was expected—even required—to "make an honest woman of her," in order to bestow kinship, honor, and legitimacy on the infant.

If the father-to-be failed to comply willingly, a shotgun wedding was usually arranged; barring this, the young man would be perceived as lacking in character and trustworthiness. His reputation and status in the community would be seriously diminished. Pregnant girls thus abandoned were sometimes banished from their homes by angry and embarrassed fathers. Occasionally, young mothers-to-be were sent to live with relatives before others in the community learned of the pregnancy. After the baby was born, however, the girl (either with or without her baby, depending upon the arrangements that had been made by the family) was expected to return home, pick herself up, and get on with her life.

Mistakes were forgiven, and even expected as a normal part of life. Consequently, it was possible for teenage, single mothers to rebuild their reputations. And children born out of wedlock were not held responsible for the circumstances under which they were conceived. After all, no child ever asked to be born. But one such mistake was the limit for the parents. Repeated out-of-wedlock births, so common in many poor communities today, were simply not tolerated. A girl who married the father of her child received more respect from others in the community. And, without a doubt, a child born in—as opposed to out of—wedlock was more firmly on the road to establishing his or her own self-respect. The community would forgive but rarely forget a major violation of its rules of conduct. In that way, its members were held accountable.

There was, of course, a downside to sacrificing personal desires and interests for the "common good." Indeed, the common good has not always been the best thing for all parties involved. All shotgun marriages did not survive. Many ended in divorce, and others survived under the stress and strain of bitterness and conflict. Consequently, many children grew up with poor role models for successful marriages and loving male-female relationships. Nevertheless, they grew up in more stable two-parent families than an alarming number of children do today.

Today, it is much harder to hold people accountable. They are more inclined to do what makes them feel good. The consequences are wide-ranging. If a woman gets pregnant out of wedlock, marriage is not necessarily the first solution she and the putative father consider; they are more inclined to be individualistic about their plight. And, unfortunately, it is not difficult to find even more striking examples of the breakdown of shame that is reflected in this kind of laissez-faire behavior. In a traditional community, it would have been shocking to hear that African American women have been known to brazenly swear and fight not only on our streets but also on television talk shows broadcast nationwide. Or that African American men call women "hos" in entertainment media that are distributed for worldwide consumption.

Today, in appallingly unprecedented numbers, there are black children who curse in front of their elders and tell their parents they hate them at the slightest whim. "Good" children refuse to give old ladies their seats on public transportation, and "bad" children snatch their purses without a qualm. The worst rob, maim, and kill; and some of them challenge old ladies to a fight just for demanding a little respect.

When I was a child, we were taught common courtesies. We respected our elders by giving them deference in any manner they demanded. If we disagreed with them, and there were many times when we did, we kept it to ourselves. We were expected, pretty much without exception, to call women "Missus" or "Miss" and men "Mister" as a sign of respect.

And, yes, we gave our seats to older people in public and private places. Failure or refusal to do so was viewed as a sign of poor home training, of not having been "raised right" by our parents—a label that no one wanted. To make matters worse for the offending child, news of bad behavior traveled fast. Parents were roundly informed of the transgression by the time the child got home, and the child would be disciplined. Our parents would actually thank whoever told them about our misdeeds.

Today, parents are more likely to warn concerned adults who intervene to mind their own business. Moreover, many adults are legitimately afraid to discipline children and teens who act with total disrespect for themselves and others because to do so might invite vile language or even physical abuse. The offending children appear to have no shame—that is, they make no acknowledgment that they take seriously the standards by which they might be measured.

In an earlier era, a teenage pregnant girl and the father of the baby felt ashamed of the fact that they were bringing a child into the world under circumstances that weren't wholly supportive of the child's welfare or their own. When a misbehaving child needed correction, parents, ashamed of the child's behavior, used corporal punishment, often physically spanking the child into submission. Churches expelled parishioners from their membership rosters if they fought or appeared drunk in public, or flaunted adulterous behavior. "Sinners" had to ask the church's forgiveness before they could come back into the fold and claim redemption. To be shunned by the group had serious consequences. Parents kept their daughters and sons from socializing with "bad guys" and "fast girls." Engaging in disrespectful behavior brought dishonor not only on the offending individual but on his or her entire family.

While I am somewhat torn with respect to my stance on some of these disciplinary measures, I cannot wholly dismiss any of them. I am opposed to corporal punishment, except in cases where it could mean the difference between a child's being seriously injured and kept safe. As for churches that expel members for having premarital sex or for committing adultery, as long as the men as well as the women are brought before the congregation for breaking the rules of conduct, I support upholding the church's standards. These standards, when viewed traditionally, suggest the assumption of responsibility on an individual's part.

Today, many people seem to want to bypass certain standards in order to see how much responsibility they can avoid. In the past, parents set high standards for themselves, so that no one would be able to say their children's poor behavior was the parents' fault. To paraphrase James Baldwin, our children rarely do what we tell them, but they always do what they see us do.

Still, I am not advocating shame as a character-builder, because there is a distinction between the shame

84

one has brought on oneself because of foolish or malicious behavior and that which was a result of circumstances over which the individual had little or no control. I remember going to school with cardboard tucked into my shoes because the soles had holes in them. One day I stepped into a puddle of water and the cardboard disintegrated and left my feet exposed. All the kids in my eighth-grade class saw my feet and knew immediately that I was wearing what one girl called "raggedy" shoes. I was so ashamed that I walked away in tears; I did not want them to know that my parents couldn't afford to buy another pair of shoes for me. Although I understood why I couldn't have new shoes, it did not stop the tears from flowing as I ran down the street toward home. I was ashamed to go back to school the next day, but I did.

From that point on, I determined that when I was an adult I would make enough money so that my own children would never have to go without adequate shoes. When I got my first job, I made sure I kept my six younger sisters and brothers, as well as my parents, outfitted in shoes and clothes. In this very positive sense, then, shame kept members of our community from behavior that caused humiliation, disgrace, or embarrassment in the community. Almost everyone valued the group's opinion, because it was the group that bestowed status and acceptance. This is still the case. Unfortunately, however, the group's values have changed.

Our elders were never perfect. They struggled with rules of conduct just as we do today. The difference is that if they made a mistake they couldn't walk away and leave the cleanup to others. The community would not have sanctioned such behavior. If they transgressed the community's rules of conduct, they did so on a smaller scale. If they got drunk on Saturday nights, for instance, they were ready to get up and go to church the next day.

Children, too, had rules of conduct. We were not allowed to "listen to grown folks' business." We could not, for instance, walk into a room and join in an adult conversation unless we were expressly invited to do so. Children had to stay with their peers, and only after they had reached late adolescence or young adulthood did they earn the right to sit with the adults. Nowadays, this right is no longer earned but seized by those who neither toiled to learn the proper ways to behave nor earned the right to be accepted into adulthood.

Adults around the world since the beginning of time have probably had similar complaints about their young, who naturally have a reckless regard for what and how adults think or feel about anything. Yet these are our children for better or worse, and it is our duty to find ways to set them on the right track.

*"Respect is a two-way street" means that respect has to be both earned and given. It carries limits and responsibilities. You achieve it through good deeds and by honorable conduct. A community worth belonging to must have standards by which it measures itself and holds its members accountable. Teach children that respect is valuable, and show them what it means. It is demonstrated by giving deference to those who have earned the right to be respected, and it is earned by measuring up to high standards.*

# The Fourth Lesson:

## *Don't Make Excuses*

$\int$ imply put, ours was a culture where passing the buck wasn't tolerated. If we didn't do well in school, for example, we were held responsible for not doing our best. Parents didn't generally go to the school to tell the teacher off or blame their child's failure on the teacher. Nor did they blame "the system"—that amorphous body that is now held responsible for all manner of failures in lieu of putting the responsibility on the shoulders of the individual, where it belongs.

If we didn't get home by curfew, we knew we had to accept the consequences, which usually meant some type of punishment. The only people who could get away with excuses, except in extraordinary circumstances, were young children, the sick, the elderly, or the mentally incompetent. The rest of us had to "take our medicine" like grown men and women.

Aunt Icie used to say, "Actions speak louder than words." She and Mother believed that actions would either lead to very good results or wreck the remainder of our days on earth. In their view, one could not buy back time. The poor decisions you made early in life would follow you forever, and the consequences would be difficult to bear. The most critical question was: Can you live with the consequences of what you have done?

Adults used to be very clear about the relationship between actions and consequences. We were not allowed to make excuses. To use a common expression, "If you go to the dance, you've got to pay the band." Many of our children do not understand this expression today, and we must teach them how to get it right while they are young, never allowing them to think of themselves as victims of circumstances that were not of their making. Adults who fell into this trap as children always find a throng of others to hold responsible for the circumstances in which they find themselves. For example, if you ask some men why they don't pay child support, they blame "the system" or "the man" (i.e., white society), or a "greedy" ex-wife or girlfriend who "doesn't understand how tough it is for the brothers." Never mind that an innocent child needs to be provided for.

Consider one of my friends who recently divorced his wife. He holds several advanced degrees and is highly respected in his field. Yet he refused to pay child support because he was angry with his ex-wife over the separation. He felt personally wounded because she wanted a divorce. At first I tried to understand why he felt so angry, but my attention quickly turned to his obligation toward his daughter.

"But your daughter carries your genes; she is part of your flesh. You helped to make her into a human being,"

I challenged. He was unmoved. His anger over the divorce outweighed his feelings of personal responsibility for his daughter's care. I tried to get this man to understand that his responsibility to his child outweighed all other considerations. I was pleased to learn a few months later that he had begun to make regular child-support payments.

To be an enduring victim is to be a person who simply refuses to be held accountable. This pattern of behavior has become increasingly common among professional athletes who get into trouble. Drugs, alcohol, out-of-wedlock paternity, adultery, misappropriation of money—you name it. Ours is now a culture of victimization. We are allowed to find a host of others whom we hold responsible for the circumstances in which we find ourselves. What is so apparent is the rush to blame someone—anyone—for our actions. For many, it is not even a defense but a cocky, arrogant stride to a podium with dozens of microphones and eager paparazzi hanging on their every word. The response is virtually scripted. Instead of hearing this person say, "I'm sorry I did wrong. I apologize to my wife, my children, my mother and father, my friends, and all those folks out there who thought I was a genuine hero," what we are more likely to hear is a pack of lies or a shifting of the burden of responsibility to any moving target. A young, gifted, but obviously out-of-control basketball player, caught with a gun and marijuana in a car in which he was a passenger, said, "The media is the problem. They're the ones who blew this up into a problem. I don't have a problem!"

I call it "the devil made me do it" defense: "No, I didn't hit her. She fell down the stairs all by herself." This response is blatant obfuscation, passing the buck big-time. Sadly, we see this same behavior in entertainers and politicians (as well as thieves and crooks), and the tragedy is that these are the people who are being held up as role models for our children. The kids would be a lot better off if we asked them to emulate the sturdy, hardworking men in their families and churches, and the stable husbands and fathers in their neighborhoods. A flashy and confused or downright immoral athlete, entertainer, or politician with big bucks to spend on frivolous things and no sense of self is precisely the kind of person we don't want our children to emulate.

We often hear accounts of people who claim they've been saved or changed their ways. Simply saying they've been redeemed wouldn't have been good enough in the old days. When offenders sought forgiveness, they didn't get off so easily. They had to work hard—continuously—to show their fellow sisters and brothers that they had indeed accepted responsibility for their actions. They couldn't fast-forward, as if they were flicking the remote control of a VCR; and they had to behave in a measured, moderate way, and try like hell to stay out of sight.

Today, we see a lot of the opposite: flaunting misbehavior; lecturing about it for hefty fees; writing books about it; and, on occasion, being rewarded with a made-for-television drama or a movie about the life of a rogue, and, in general, profiting from irresponsible and immoral behavior.

Obviously, this is not exclusively a black issue. From the highest levels of government to the churches, from the schools to the civic clubs and civil rights organizations, leaders are abdicating responsibility for their wrongdoing. How many more times do we have to be subjected to men copping a plea with their long-suffering wives by their side?

Children in my generation could not have imagined such a scene. No bad news was expected to come to our parents about our behavior. Virtually any adult could and would inform our parents about any misbehavior they saw us engaging in. If we sneaked off and went to the

# 10

# The Fifth Lesson:

## *Do an Honest Day's Work*

Dr. Martin Luther King Jr. once said, "If a man is called to be a street sweeper, he should sweep streets even as Michelangelo painted, or Beethoven composed music, or Shakespeare wrote poetry. He should sweep streets so well that all the hosts of heaven and earth will pause to say, Here lived a great street sweeper who did his job well." Yet the myth of the Lazy Negro has dominated popular culture and lore for generations. I cannot emphasize strongly enough how far this myth is from the truth.

We lived on my stepfather's meager salary of about $30 dollars a week, from which he paid $15 dollars a month for child support for his two children from a previous marriage. Yet we children did not resort to stealing, prostitution, or selling illegal liquor (Mississippi was a dry state) in order to get what we needed or wanted. We found baby-sitting jobs, cleaned white people's homes on Saturdays, bagged groceries at the local store, and picked cotton to get money for school clothes. If we couldn't find a legal way to make enough money to get these things, we were taught to be resourceful enough to make do with what we had or to accept the fact that we would not die from having to do without.

If my strength was born in my parents' home, my resolve was born in the homes of the white folks whose houses I cleaned on Saturdays to get spending money—$2.50 to $3 for a full day's work. There were no McDonald's fast-food restaurants that hired teenagers. Even though being consigned to this type of work was a painful lesson that I had to get an education so I could do more with my life than clean and cook, I did the job: It was a means to an end.

"Hard work," all the older people said at one time or another, "never killed nobody."

In times of prosperity and times of scarcity, the labor of blacks has been a persistent feature of American life. Slaves were rarely compensated for their labor. The slaveholders provided them with a wooden shack to live in and the simplest food to eat, but little else. Still, our forebears produced the cotton crops and built the plantations in the South. They helped build the cities in the North. Their entire lives were organized to produce as much as they possibly could for a rapidly developing economy from which they derived no benefit.

The great migration North brought masses to the cities of St. Louis, Chicago, Detroit, Milwaukee, Los Angeles, and New York, where they found work in factories in the newly industrializing America. For the most part, however, job opportunities were severely restricted, but that did not quench blacks' desire to work and achieve the American dream.

There was no such thing as unacceptable work then, because blacks usually didn't have alternatives. They were simply glad to get a job at all. Without the opportunity to get a formal education, most blacks had little to barter for subsistence. Work was the key to being honest, meeting one's family obligations, assuming personal responsibility for one's own upkeep, and making a contribution to one's village of neighbors. The only line my parents drew on the type of job they did was whether it was honest.

Today, there is a rapidly transforming economy that requires greater technical competence. And new immigrants from Asia and South America are eagerly taking the unskilled and semiskilled jobs that blacks often turn down. Our attitudes toward work seem to have changed. I challenge parents to teach their children to take any job they can get. Young people shouldn't feel that they must start at the top with their first jobs. Work that would be considered menial today did not affect our self-esteem in an adverse way.

"Nothing is more important than an honest day's work, " Mother said. She taught her five daughters that we should become economically independent, because we might have to take care of ourselves one day. This showed great prescience, because all of us have divorced and have spent some time as single parents. Mother also told all of her children that work makes you self-reliant, and it makes you feel important. And she warned, "No one likes to associate with a lazy person who has no ambition to succeed in life."

A ditchdigger could earn as much respect as a doctor in her eyes. There was no such thing as looking down on people who worked in unskilled "dirty" jobs, because it was the honesty of one's efforts that measured success. Of course, doctors were looked up to not just because they were doctors but because they had worked hard and long to get where they were and there were so few of such people. My town had two doctors, one dentist, a host of teachers, a handful of funeral directors, and a lot of preachers. The preachers whose congregations were large enough to take care of them and those cited above constituted the fledging middle class, which was not large enough to form a separate elite.

Black doctors formed networks among themselves that reached beyond the towns and states in which they lived. It was not unusual for them to send their children to prestigious black institutions, and to the Seven Sisters colleges and Ivy League universities. Some went away to boarding school as well, particularly to Northfield Mt. Hermon in Massachusetts, and to the all-black Palmer Institute in North Carolina. These institutions provided the black upper class with a powerful national network, and many of these relationships last to this day.

But the doctor, the maid, and the ditchdigger belonged to the same church, which was usually Baptist and occasionally Methodist, Presbyterian, or Catholic. There were so few in the upper class that they could not segregate themselves in their own neighborhoods, as is the custom today. They usually sent their children to the same schools and lived in the same neighborhoods as those who were less educated and therefore less prosperous. As a result, the deacon or the trustee in the church may well have been the ditchdigger, and the maid may have been the church secretary. They, no less than the doctor, also had considerable status in the eyes of their family and friends, for they held highly respected roles in a valued institution. They used their lowly jobs to achieve upward mobility. They bought or built homes, educated their children, and, when possible, put a little money away in savings.

They stretched their low wages farther than seemed humanly possible. My stepfather's mother, Grandmother

Ida, worked for many years as a maid to a white family, the Baldwins, who owned a furniture store. She was never paid more than $3 per day plus bus fare. It therefore came as a shock even to her family when we learned that she had saved enough to send my cousin to nursing school, even though my cousin chose not to go. Grandmother Ida was the kind of ordinary hero that Martin Luther King Jr. would have respected.

*"Do an honest day's work" means appreciating the way our forebears turned hard work into opportunities for achievement. Success begins with the initiative to get a job, and then doing the very best you can with it. Honest work makes you feel good about your ability to accomplish something useful. It gives structure and order to life. We put pride aside if we ever need to choose between pride and an honest paycheck that will make us self-reliant.*

# 11

# The Sixth Lesson:

## *Make a Way Out of No Way*

When I was a little girl, Mother used to make soap. It was usually in the fall, after the heat of summer had subsided and before it got too cold. For months Mother dutifully collected all of the grease dripping from her cooking and from that of our grandmother and great-aunt, who lived a few yards from us. Out in the backyard, Mother would start a big fire under her round cast iron pot, which had turned black from years of use.

She would pour all the grease dripping into the pot, add some water, then add a can of the highly poisonous "devil's lye," which she warned us to stay away from because it would burn your skin off upon contact. After these ingredients had boiled for a while, she would let the mixture cool off. Then she cut large bars of soap, wrapped them in newspaper, and put them away until it was time to use them to wash clothes. For bathing, we used store-bought Ivory or Cashmere Bouquet.

Mother came from a cultural tradition of what I call doers. It was a tradition evolved by women and men who learned to perform any task or to get any job done, no matter what it was. Because of their circumstances, it appeared that they didn't have the means to get the job done, but they simply worked with what they had. Moreover, their family and friends were in the same boat. These women and men not only made their own soap; they grew their own vegetables and fruit, and canned their homegrown produce for the winter. They raised cows and hogs, ground peanuts for peanut butter, and the men hunted wild game and fished to assure a well-rounded, if simple, diet.

Neighbors borrowed sugar from neighbors, exchanged baby-sitting duties, sponsored fish fries to raise money to build new churches, sold sweet-potato pies and coconut cakes to send their children to black colleges, and sponsored rent parties in Harlem or on Chicago's South Side. They did all of these things and more to ensure the security and survival of their communities and their members. Black folks knew that they had to do whatever was called for to "make it."

These resourceful habits reflected a tradition of "making a way out of no way." One had to be as inventive as possible. The necessities of life were not the only things early African Americans learned to develop. Indeed, some went on to become inventors. George Washington Carver of the Tuskegee Institute in Alabama, for example, developed hundreds of products that were derived from the common peanut.

Our ancestors were brought up to believe that they could do anything, and they learned how. Fending for themselves, which they did much earlier than we do today, required them to have high personal standards and many different skills. They had to develop a great deal of flexibility. They had to learn how to do a lot of things simultaneously, and to do them well. I was taught, for instance—not only by my parents but also in home economics class at school—to wash, cook, sew, set the table, and iron clothes. All of us had to learn these skills. They were meant to help us become self-sufficient in adulthood. We were also made aware of the historical tradition that we were following: that of men and women who had little but nevertheless organized schools and colleges, homes for the aged, lodges, churches, clubs, and orphanages.

A doer used whatever was available to get a job done. As Mother used to say, "If you don't have the horse, ride the cow." If unexpected guests arrived, we found enough food to share with them.

A doer responded spontaneously to any need. For instance, there were many times when one of our neighbors' homes caught fire and burned to the ground. The small frame houses were highly flammable and the only fire station was downtown, at least four miles away. In addition, the family often had no telephone to call the fire department hastily. We accepted the reality that if our house caught on fire, it was most likely to burn to the ground and the occupants probably wouldn't be able to save any of their possessions. Everyone joined together to help them get back on their feet, sometimes overnight. We went door-to-door to collect money, bed linen, mattresses, clothes, shoes, pots and pans, food, and, most of all, a place for the distressed family to stay.

Whenever I read a story today about Habitat for Humanity or how the Amish come together to build a house for one of their brethren, I am reminded of the countless times I saw the folks in Palmers dish out their generosity to one another. In our community, reciprocity was a form of social insurance. For example, if I help you when your house burns down, I can expect you to help me if I have a misfortune. This is my way of ensuring that I will not be left alone to fend for myself in my greatest hour of need.

Our needs were frequent and would by today's standards be considered serious and costly. They included raising money to bury the dead who had no burial insurance, helping to pay the medical bills of the uninsured, buying food for the unemployed, and so on. Since none of us had a lot, we shared what we did have. There were few incentives to be selfish because our security was found within the group.

We were also challenged to be creative in the use of our scarce resources. For example, a baseball could be made from fabric by wrapping it as densely as possible until it became a firm, hard object; rag dolls were made from scraps of fabric (or scraps were used for a quilt top); and musical instruments were fashioned from tin cans or by whittling a piece of wood for a wind instrument. Our clothes were more homemade than store-bought, though we naturally preferred the ones from the department store. Most girls learned to sew in home economics classes or were taught by their mothers.

Mother said her parents used to take the cloth sacks from the meal and flour they purchased in bulk. After they were washed and bleached, Grandma Martha made dresses for her five girls and shirts for her six boys. They rarely got store-bought or "Sunday clothes" (i.e., clothes one wore to church or on other special occasions).

By the time Mother had us, she didn't have to use feed sacks to make our clothes. Instead, she purchased fabric to make each of her five girls a dress, or we got the occasional store-bought dresses and shoes. The residents of our community were so homogeneous that no one was in any position to criticize anyone else.

I suppose there were times when Mother and her sisters and brothers were ashamed that they had so few clothes, but two things helped to minimize their embarrassment. First, practically all the families they knew used the same feed sacks to make clothes. Second, there was no community pressure, as there is today, to wear the latest name-brand fashions. Simply put, Calvin Klein did not have his name emblazoned on the back of a pair of blue jeans. As a result, people didn't sit at home and feel sorry for themselves because they were poor. Being poor was a fact of life, but it wasn't a state of being.

I feel that it was because our ancestors were able to project their hopes and aspirations for a better life onto their children and their generation that they were able to keep going. They were fully committed to envisioning a prosperous future for the next generation if their own was not able to pull it off. Deferred gratification was probably not that difficult, especially in view of the fact that their immediate ancestors had come out of such a dark and brutal past.

Another precondition for being a doer was that you couldn't be overwhelmed by the enormity of a task. For my parents and their generation, no undertaking was too small or too great, and no reward was too minimal. Surely if Harriet Tubman had been overwhelmed many blacks would have remained in slavery instead of escaping as they did. Uneducated parents would not have been able to figure out how to take little scraps of opportunities and weave them into a successful set of opportunities to send their kids to college. Many elderly men and women did what would by today's standards be considered demeaning work in order to send their kids to college. As we go in search of role models for our young today, we would do well to hark back to the days when we were surrounded by them.

Finally, being a doer was like eating and sleeping. Figuring out how to get things done was a normal part of life, not something that we tucked to the side and reserved for a project or a special volunteer activity. In this way, children grew accustomed to being able to reach within themselves to find the will to develop the skills they needed to meet their needs.

The contrast to children today is stark. They have grown up as consumers instead of as doers. Many believe that they must buy the most expensive jeans, advertising someone else's name on their backside; they must have the latest sneakers, preferably by Michael Jordan and costing in excess of $100; and they want the latest jackets, shirts, and expensive designer sunglasses. We learned early how to do without things. Our children, who are quick to turn up their noses at no-name clothes and sneakers, don't appreciate us buying them old cars. They measure their identity and self-worth by the children whose parents buy new cars.

My parents would have thought I had lost my mind if I had rejected an article of clothing they gave me for Christmas because one of my classmates had one that was more expensive. We didn't have the vast range of options that our children now have. Greater options, however, do not necessarily make for more informed, educated, or enlightened individuals. The opposite can occur. If a child has too many things, he or she may make poor choices and never understand how to sacrifice, how to suffer a little, how to want something very badly but not be able to get it. This kind of experience can create fortitude and stimulate creativity (i.e., promote the development of resourcefulness). I feel that all of these responses are character-builders.

When I think of these issues in relation to my young-adult son, I wish I had another chance to parent again, because I could have insisted that he learn to do a lot more on his own behalf. Children need the chance to shoulder responsibilities and make important decisions and critical choices. It is no wonder that so many middle-class young adults return home to live with their parents after they finish college. We have trained them to expect to have all the things they want immediately. They do not know how to defer gratification until they can work to earn the money they need to purchase the expensive item they want. And we are all too eager to subsidize them when they ask for our help.

I have always been surprised at the large number of freshman students who come to Howard University with brand-new cars that their parents have bought them. They also bring microwave ovens, televisions and VCRs, stereos, and just about anything else they are accustomed to having at home.

I do not mean to indict all of our young adults, only to point to the problems that a significant number of them may be facing. They do not know as much as they should or need to know about relying on their own inner resources to solve their problems. Many black children grow up without ever learning to tap the resources and power within themselves. They are encouraged by their parents and the media to externalize everything. By projecting their needs outward, and by looking to others for solutions, they lose countless opportunities to develop their inherent capacities and their power to understand the problems and issues that beset them.

Resourceful people are usually attuned to their own needs and abilities at an early age and can exert charisma, at times, to encourage others to join their team of worker bees, using skill, excitement, and a singular focus on what they have to get done. They believe they can get the job done, and they aren't likely to give up if they fail on the first try. Individuals with less enthusiasm, drive, and initiative are more likely to be resourceless.

*"Making a way out of no way" means being resourceful, developing coping skills, and tapping the power within to get the job done. These are lifelong endeavors, so continue to challenge yourself throughout your life—and never give up! You can never learn enough, nor can you learn too much. You make continuous improvement in your skills, and you should keep a regular inventory of new activities to which you hope to apply these skills.*

*Today, we do not have to make lye soap, stitch our own quilts, or sew clothes from cheap fabric. But we, no less than earlier generations of doers, face numerous challenges that require all the coping skills we can muster.*

# 12

# The Seventh Lesson:
## *Every Child Can Learn*

My youngest aunt finished the ninth grade, and that was a cause for jubilation in Mother's large family. My biological father went to Piney Woods boarding school in Mississippi for a time but did not finish because he had to go to work. They represented a generation of African Americans in the North and the South who had nursed dreams of achieving an education themselves but had lacked the opportunity. So they passed their hopes on to their children.

They viewed education as a set of intangible skills. Once you got an education, they were fond of saying, it was yours to keep for the rest of your life. No one could take it from you. You didn't have to worry about being exploited without just compensation. Exploitation was common. For example, my father never received vacations, sick leave, or the retirement pension that white workers received. He retired on Social Security. Our education was supposed to lift us up from second-class citizenship. It would be the ultimate measure of our parents' success.

We kids talked to one another about our elders' dashed dreams and limited opportunities, and felt that we had a special responsibility not to let them down. Mother reminded us often that she would have studied nursing but she didn't have the opportunity. "You children have the opportunity that I wish I'd had," she said. "You have no excuse not to get an education." All of our parents wanted and expected us to be better off than they were. By contrast, my son's generation will be the first black generation in which many children will be worse off than their parents are.

Our parents' dreams arose from events that changed the nation and the world. African American men fought in World War II for "freedom abroad" but were denied the most basic civil rights, such as the right to vote, when they returned home. Instead, what they found was that the expanding economic opportunities taking place across the nation did not benefit them equally in the North and did not benefit them at all in the segregated South. Thus many of these veterans became the clandestine organizers of the National Association for the Advancement of Colored People (NAACP) throughout the South. Human dignity, they affirmed, would come to their children, if not to them. In 1954, the United States Supreme Court found segregated schools in *Brown v. Board of Education* to be illegal. The ruling outlawed the segregation of public education. The Montgomery, Alabama, bus boycott led by Martin Luther King Jr. fueled their passion for racial equality, as did outrage over lynchings.

The Mississippi Board of Higher Education also started

paying the tuition for black students to attend out-of-state universities if they wanted to study a subject (i.e., medicine, dentistry, engineering, or law) that was not offered at one of the state-supported black colleges. The education of many physicians was subsidized at Meharry Medical College, Howard University, and other medical schools by the state government because the officials had no intention of integrating the all-white University of Mississippi.

Meanwhile, in Africa, the children of our ancestors had begun to successfully wage wars of independence against their European colonizers. Countries such as Kenya and Ghana served as role models for some of our parents, who felt that we here in this country could do no less than our brothers and sisters in Africa. Politically sensitive African Americans looked to Africa as a source of pride and dignity and hope, in spite of the fact that the American media's coverage of the African continent amounted to little more than images of Tarzan subduing or leading a tribe of fear-stricken or worshipful natives. The sight of Jomo Kenyatta ousting the British imperialists provided an extraordinary counterpoint to these images. Education was considered essential to increasing our political awareness and participation; after all, our parents envisioned us as civic leaders and elected officials. We shared our parents' vision, and they shared ours, which was much simpler but equally compelling. While education was not a cure-all, it was clearly the most viable antidote to spending the rest of our days in a small southern community "going nowhere."

My school had hand-me-down textbooks, two or three glass burners for what passed as a science lab, and a dirt court for our competitive basketball games. One of my teachers, Mrs. Zola Jackson, who doubled as the school librarian, was one of those committed teachers from the old school. Apparently, she had always been a high achiever, odds and obstacles be damned. And she expected no less of her students. I remember her telling us how as a child she had listened to classical music and sometimes studied while washing dishes or doing other chores. She had attended Rust College, which was originally called Shaw University, when it was started by the Freedmen's Bureau shortly after the end of the Civil War.

During her years as a teacher, Mrs. Jackson was adamant about improving herself. In the summers, our teachers took courses at such places as the historically black Alcorn State University and Jackson State University in Mississippi. Some of them even went to places like Indiana University and Columbia University's Teachers College. I believe my teachers were required to eventually earn a bachelor's degree, but they were allowed to start teaching without one. Some of them went on to earn their master's degree.

When I was growing up, as had been the case since emancipation, teaching was the most respectable and feasible profession for a black woman. I do not doubt that some of my teachers were frustrated and felt stifled, and knew, as was probably true, that if they were given a chance they could excel in other professions; still, they cast down their buckets where they were and gave teaching all they had. My teachers, the majority of whom were women, were all as industrious and enthusiastic about learning as they were about teaching. Almost all of these women had husbands and children and other obligations in addition to their jobs, but they still found a way to further their education. It was in their pursuit of higher education that people like Mrs. Jackson were exposed to or cultivated their interest in classical music, opera, and "serious" theater. It was no wonder that Mrs. Bernice Newman, a 4-H club agent, could teach my sister Dorie how to sing the title song from *La Traviata* for a high school contest, or that Miss Janet Dozier could give

Carolyn Hales, my classmate, voice lessons and the kind of mentorship that allowed her to win statewide operatic contests and to aspire to go to The Juilliard School to study opera.

Though our schools were materially unequal to those of our white peers, it was much easier for us to excel back then, because our teachers were genuinely concerned with our learning and believed our scholastic achievement was tied to the continued progress of the race. The assumption was that we *could* learn, that we *would* learn, and if they failed in their efforts to teach us, they considered it a sign of their own inadequacy. There was no such thing as a child's being "uneducable." My teachers let students know that it was unacceptable to be dumb, to be "trifling" when it came to schoolwork. What a tragedy, what an abomination it is that today our boys and girls are ridiculed for their academic excellence and ranked on for "tryna be white." To equate scholastic excellence with trying to be white is a horror, but it is the corollary that is far more insidious. As others have pointed out, if being smart is being white, then being dumb is being black.

Being dumb gained you no medals when I was growing up. It didn't make you popular one whit. In fact, teachers often had to chastise the smart kids for teasing the slower students. If we did, we were punished either by having to stay in the classroom to do chores during recess or by having to stand in the corner on one leg. And if our parents found out what we had done, they punished us again when we got home. Compassion was just one of the values our teachers instilled in us. The majority of our teachers heartily took on the role of surrogate parents, and it was not a role that I or my peers questioned. That was just the way things were.

Today, the rewards for being "dumb" are, for many children and youths, greater than those for being "smart." The rap-music culture, for example, compensates the artists who glorify and celebrate ghetto culture with lucrative recording contracts and the like. The vilification of black women by rap artists and the youths who emulate them represents a complete turnaround in the culture of poor blacks. No one in Palmers, including the "bad people," would have rewarded the youths who imitate rap artists by calling women "bitches," "sluts," and "whores." Mrs. Jackson would literally have washed their mouths out with soap and water, proceeded to their homes before they themselves got there and told their parents, who would have beaten the living daylights out of them. Whether you are for or against corporal punishment today, it certainly would have been a deterrent to such ill-mannered, downright vile behavior back then.

Like parents, our teachers were not perfect. Some, though good teachers, just weren't very good people. Then, as now, we had to contend with teachers who had pet pupils. Being the teacher's pet meant getting sent on errands to the principal's office or to other classrooms, getting the leading roles in school plays, and having special privileges in class. If you were a smart, nice kid you were virtually assured of being the teacher's pet. Sometimes it was based on work and behavior, but often it was a matter of class. Indifference was your punishment for being poor. I vowed that I would never draw a line between the haves and the have-nots, especially among children. Then, as now, warm, caring teachers like Mrs. Jackson were precious.

A few years ago, one of my former teachers told me that Mrs. Jackson had a budget of about $100 a year to buy books for the entire school. The budget was set by the Forrest County Board of Education, an all-white body that granted the white schools a book budget of perhaps ten times what was allowed for the schools in the black district. Our library consisted of a bookshelf in Mrs. Jackson's classroom. Its holdings included a set of encyclopedias, a few history books and biographies of such famous blacks as Paul Robeson, W. E. B. Du Bois, and Oscar De Priest, who had served in the U.S. Congress during Reconstruction, and for whom our school had been named. One of the books I remember marveling at was *For My People,* by Margaret Walker. Mrs. Jackson had told us that Margaret Walker had become famous with that little book of poetry, a fact I would remember when I saw Professor Margaret Walker walking across campus at Jackson State College when I was a freshman there.

Mrs. Jackson was the first intellectual I ever knew. Of course, at that time I didn't have a full grasp of what it meant to be an intellectual, but I remember thinking that she was different from most of the other teachers, because she made me feel that learning wasn't merely necessary but precious, exciting. This was most apparent in her passion for reading and her constant encouragement of her students to read books beyond what was assigned in class. Dorie and I were among the students who caught Mrs. Jackson's reading fever, and when she recognized this she habitually passed on to us every new book that came into the school library. I will always remember the time Dorie and I graduated to the level where Mrs. Jackson introduced us to a thick volume with a navy-blue cover: a history of western civilization. Dorie read it from beginning to end within a few days; she was the faster reader. When she passed the book on to me, I followed suit, but it took me a lot longer to get through it. It was my first window onto the vast, wide world.

As far as our parents were concerned, the teacher was always right. Teachers were part of our all-black, self-reliant but interdependent communities. I have always felt that one of the reasons our teachers were so successful at being resourceful—at doing so much with so little—was that they lived in, and were an integral part of, our communities. Our teachers' values were the same as those of our parents, extended family, neighbors, and church members, and were the foundation for teacher effectiveness, student outcomes, as well as parent and community participation. The uniformity in values gave rise to high expectations for our educational success, and there was little disagreement between our parents and our teachers.

These shared values were based on the aspirations of the common culture of an oppressed people, and on an enduring respect for teachers and the profession of teaching. Our parents entrusted us to our teachers' care because they had great respect for their formal training, credibility, integrity, honesty, and the high expectations they, too, held for us.

Increasingly, studies of urban secondary schooling note the connection between a school's effectiveness and the consistent and shared values of both academic excellence and sound discipline. I recognize that in a diverse society it is difficult to have uniform values and expectations in public schools. The racial integration of schools and neighborhoods, not only between whites and African Americans but also with rapidly growing populations of Hispanics and Asians in particular, complicates our expectations for uniform values. Public schools must observe a string of bureaucratic and legal requirements that do not exist in private schools. Shared values and standards today are based on academic excellence, discipline, and respect for authority rather than on the race or ethnicity of a particular group.

However, many of the private schools started by black parents since the reforms of the sixties—the Marva Collins schools in the poor inner-city neighborhoods of Chicago, for example, and countless others—have effectively provided an education that is based on many of the traditional African American values and expectations.

During my generation, the dedication of our teachers

was also rooted in their expectation that there should be generation succession. They worked hard to train us to be ready to take up the reins of leadership and good citizenship roles in our segregated black communities. I had several high school teachers who were members of the largely underground NAACP, which was outlawed in most of the Deep South. Their commitment to racial justice was dangerous, because they were fired, run out of town, or killed if it became known that they were members of a civil rights organization. Despite the risks, they tried to instill in us enough of a social conscience to enable us to become the generation that would break down the walls of racial segregation.

Their silent witness to social justice was not lost on us, for many of them became the role models for our civil rights activism in the 1960s. I can recall repeated examples of teachers giving us the aid and comfort we needed as student activists—sometimes overt, sometimes covert. Even though many of us ended up living in the urban North instead of the South, I would like to think that the teachers who taught us in the North and the South wanted us, most of all, to be successful in our work, to have good character and a social conscience

Respect for teachers and the profession of teaching began to decline among African Americans in the late sixties and early seventies when other occupations began to open up for us. I have visited countless public schools around the country, and, sadly, they are often a microcosm of what is wrong in our society. Teachers are now expected to fill critical roles that used to be carried out by the "village that raised the children." In schools across the nation, teachers are no longer the authority figures in their classrooms. Violent and disruptive students, disrespectful parents, and a hostile public challenge this power to the point where students now attack teachers verbally and physically. The declining respect for authority in the wider society is a related cause of this development.

As citizens, we have demonstrated the value we assign to our teachers in the most telling way possible: the low pay they receive. Teachers make less than accountants, lawyers, doctors, and preachers. Nor should we be surprised when teachers who should be instructing our children on gene-splicing and cell and molecular biology are merely dissecting frogs in the laboratory because of our inadequate investment in equipment, new schools, and the proper teacher training. Given the paltry investment we make in our children's education, it is not surprising that many young people enter the workforce without the skills necessary to function in a highly competitive technological society. Effective teachers are those who have the required skills to transmit the new knowledge base to their students. These teachers are the pivotal link between our children, ourselves, and the future that we want our children to have.

Last year, at my aunt and uncle LeDrester and Eddie James Hayes's fiftieth-anniversary celebration, I met Miss Ola, as she is called in Hattiesburg. Throughout the nation she is known as Osceola McCarty, the eighty-year-old black woman who recently endowed a scholarship fund for black students at the University of Southern Mississippi with a gift of $150,000. She had accumulated this sum after years of working as a washerwoman for Hattiesburg's white families. Miss Ola, a close friend of my aunt's family, is a diminutive, soft-spoken, very gentle woman who speaks through her animated eyes. She had lived practically all of her life in Hattiesburg as a simple, God-fearing woman who never married. Miss Ola had also nursed a lifelong desire for an education. That opportunity had eluded her when she was forced to drop out of school in the sixth grade and begin working because of her mother's illness.

As time went on, it was clear that she would not be able to return to school. So she worked hard and saved most of her meager earnings. She lived simply, in an immaculate small frame house that had neither air-conditioning nor a color television. Even her treasured Bible, which she read daily, had almost fallen apart. Miss Ola's frugal lifestyle was also expressed in her simple starched and ironed cotton dresses, and the "Old Lady Comfort" lace-up black shoes that she had cut on the sides to relieve the pain of bunions.

A teller at the local bank brought it to the attention of the bank president that Miss Ola had accumulated hundreds of thousands of dollars, an extraordinary sum for a washerwoman. The bank president wanted to know what she intended to do with this money. She said that she had always wanted an education but had been too poor to get one, so she wanted to help the "colored boys and girls" get a college education. He set up a meeting between Miss Ola and his former college classmate, Aubrey Lucas, who was now the president of the University of Southern Mississippi. They appealed to her to establish an endowment for black students studying at the hometown university. Once she agreed, the bank president laid out several dimes before her and asked her to allocate how many she wanted to contribute to scholarships, as her personal gift to her pastor and her cousin, and, of course, as money to live on. She allocated most of the dimes for the scholarship program, some for the pastor of her church and her cousin, and the balance as living expenses for the remainder of her life.

Miss Ola symbolizes the best of the values of a generation of people who were denied the opportunity to secure an education for themselves but have always worked hard to open doors for the young. That generation has now left the job to us. Unless we do our part, the doors will slowly close.

*"Every child can learn" means that you believe in everyone's potential, including your own. You unlock this potential with a sense of purpose; the ability to envision a future as a successful person; the ability to set and achieve goals; a strengthened identity; a measure of dignity; and, most important, survival skills, which include a relevant education.*

*Young people need the strength of will, the toughness of character, the power to resist needless temptations, the ability to endure in the face of intractable obstacles, and the power to maintain their special human capacity to learn even in the face of evil—a term academics rarely use. In so doing, they will be able to pass something of enormous benefit on to the next generation. Only when we—as equal partners with their teachers—do our part to help these children, will we have returned to our true mission.*

# 13

# The Eighth Lesson:
## *Keep the Can-Do Spirit*

I remember the day clearly. It was in early December. I was lying in my bed at Barnes Hospital, the institution operated by Washington University in St. Louis, where I was a graduate student. It was a full day after I had had surgery for the removal of an ovarian cyst caused by the painful disease endometriosis. My doctor, Frank Long Jr., walked into my room and said, "Get up. You've got studying to do." He took one of my textbooks from my nightstand and put the book in my lap.

"You've got to keep up with your studies while you're here," he said. "Sickness is no excuse for not doing your work." I looked at him a bit dumbfounded. Didn't he realize that I had just had my abdomen cut open and was in the worst pain of my life?

"I can't study," I said. "I can't even cough without my stomach feeling like it's ripping apart." I got no sympathy from this tall, thin white man with jet-black hair and a pleasant, upbeat demeanor.

"You can do it," he said. "You're tough. I've known you were going to succeed since the first time you came to my office."

Dr. Long reminded me, at that moment, of my mother and father, both of whom had a strong can-do spirit. "It's not important that you fall down," they said to us kids repeatedly, "but that you dust yourself off and get back up and keep going." They had little tolerance for people who complained a lot, especially about minor things they could fix. "Stop whining," my dad commanded when we kids complained incessantly about something. "People get tired of hearing someone complain all the time. Do something to fix your problem, then you won't have to complain," he often said. Dr. Long was cut from the same cloth, I thought. Each time a problem confronted my parents, they found a way to bounce right back. They would have expected me to get back on my feet as quickly as I could. Much of their resilience was forged in the throes of stark economic deprivation, which required them to keep functioning in the midst of adversity.

"Don't expect anything to be handed to you on a silver platter," Mother chided us. "Colored people don't have the luxury of wallowing in our problems or thinking about ourselves all the time. I want you children to learn how to handle just about anything that happens."

Dr. Long would perform surgery on me for endometriosis two more times during the next three years. I would end up with a total of six surgeries for this disease, which afflicts hundreds of thousands of women. Each time I was hospitalized, it was my parents' teachings and Dr. Long's cheerleading that tapped the power within me to transcend the awful pain and focus on accomplishing my goal of getting a doctorate in sociology. I also had a wonderful support group that included my adviser, Lee Rainwater, a distinguished sociologist, and my friends, who were also in the doctoral sociology program. They included Gwen Jones, my roommate from North Carolina; Ethel Sawyer, my sorority sister from Tougaloo College; her roommate, Janice Jackson, a Mississippian who attended Tougaloo and was a high school science teacher in St. Louis; and Boone Hammond, who was married and had five children even while attending graduate school full-time.

My friends were young, energetic, success-oriented, and optimistic about the world that lay before them. Their parents had taught them the same lessons Mother and Daddy Bill had taught us—to strive hard to achieve, to have faith in our own abilities, to always find a way to solve our own problems, and, most of all, to bounce back. If you couldn't do it alone, there were friends and family who could help. They helped me.

I have carried this optimism, reassurance, and can-do spirit with me through a life that has seen both tragedies and triumphs. The older I get, the more important I find these virtues to be; they have become indelibly etched in my spirit. I have taught my son, my younger sisters and brothers, and my students that no matter how many times you're knocked down, the important thing is to get up, even though I often marvel at the fact that God places more burdens on some of our people than we think they can or should have to bear.

Think of the many tragedies that beset Betty Shabazz, the widow of Malcolm X. She had to raise six daughters alone following his assassination. Despite this tragedy, she went back to graduate school and earned a doctorate degree, became a college administrator, and found the time to rehabilitate her husband's image in the minds of Americans and other people throughout the world. She bounced back and kept getting stronger, demonstrating a remarkable amount of resilience. Still, tragedy continued to befall her. One of her daughters was arrested for allegedly trying to hire a hit man to assassinate Louis Farrakhan, who Shabazz and her daughter felt was responsible for Malcolm's death. After her daughter was rehabilitated and the charges against her were dropped, the daughter's troubled twelve-year-old son set Shabazz's apartment ablaze, causing her to suffer third-degree burns over 80 percent of her body. The final misfortune claimed her life. Her life is a shining example of righteousness.

"Been Down So Long, Seems Like Up to Me" is the title of an old Negro spiritual that speaks to this virtue. Being knocked down is nothing new to black people, but manifold numbers of our young and elderly alike are finding it more and more difficult to get up off the ground for several reasons.

The routine misfortunes the average family experiences today are more complex than those they experienced in the past, and it is far more difficult to find friends or family to lend a helping hand. When I was a child, I went from our home to my grandparents', to our great-aunt and great-uncle's, and along the way I would stop at the houses of Miss Katie and her husband, Pa Joe, and Mr. and Miss Moseley, because we all lived within yards of each other. I would sit and talk to them, run errands, or find some other pastime to keep myself occupied.

These relationships relieved the pressure of intense one-on-one interaction with my mother. Having an extended family also took some of the pressure off my mother and father as they struggled to raise eight children. One of these assortments of adults in our modified family compound was always looking out for us, observing signs that might serve as early warnings that we were headed for trouble. Today, unfortunately, families may not only lack a support network, but be potentially at risk in ways that are largely unprecedented.

Even the children of the secure middle class have their share of troubles. One of my longtime girlfriends described her two daughters as being "fragile and less sure of what they want to do with their lives." Even though they have finished college, she said, "the smallest thing seems to throw them for a loop and they get defeated so easily. They don't know how to bounce back like we did when we were their age."

Perhaps this is because we didn't teach them how to be resilient. We shouldered so many of their problems that we didn't give them the opportunity to experience the bumps in the road that would have helped them to develop a capacity for resilience. How can they pick themselves up after a fall if we always rush to the scene to save them? In effect, we may have crippled them by snatching away the opportunities they needed to cultivate their coping skills. We did this because we did not want them to suffer the way we did. And yet we inadvertently caused our children to miss one of life's most valuable lessons.

The tradition of resilience is needed more now than at any other time in recent history. One of the best examples of resilience I have ever encountered is the life of the late civil rights activist Fannie Lou Hamer, who frequently told her audiences that she was "sick and tired of being sick and tired."

Hamer was the youngest of twenty-one children in her Mississippi sharecropper family. Her life was marked by one tragedy after another. She limped when she walked because she had polio as a child. She had surgery to remove a lump from her abdomen only to find that the white doctor had given her a hysterectomy without her knowledge. Her adopted daughter died of malnutrition, and she battled breast cancer during the last years of her life. In 1964, she made a memorable speech at the Democratic National Convention in which she pleaded with the delegates to unseat the racist all-white Mississippi delegation and seat the integrated delegation of civil rights activists. Although she suffered one defeat after another, she had just about the strongest faith in the love of God and the power of redemption of anyone I've ever met. Her battles caused her to get weary, but she always reminded the poor blacks with whom she worked that she was "in no ways tired," and would never abandon her struggle for civil rights for her fellow black Mississippians.

Here was a woman who always looked to the future with an unwavering optimism, and the assurance that people have the ability to solve most of their problems themselves. Fannie Lou Hamer often chided those who gave up instead of fighting their entrenched problems.

The lesson Fannie Lou Hamer taught me and my fellow 1960s civil rights activists is a lesson worth teaching today to the new generation, which does not seem to know its inner strength. Families that are not resilient have become dependent on social workers, judges, parole officers, educators, and every manner of social-service program to extricate them from their difficulties. People who would, perhaps, have functioned on their own in the past—with the help of family and friends—have traded in their independence and problem-solving abilities for entry in social-service programs that they hope will solve many of their problems for them.

The result is that some children have as many as five

different social workers, who have taken over the parenting functions, decided which school they should attend, and who their doctor and psychologist will be. Scores of adults have also surrendered authority and control over their lives to paid enablers who are supposed to help them to get back on their feet. It is ironic that they have allowed self-confidence and faith in their own abilities to erode, since much of the help that is given does not significantly change anything. What usually happens is that the paid helpers do not so much "cure" as "maintain" the poor and the troubled.

The culture of dependency must and will be broken. The government has already begun dismantling it with the so-called welfare-reform legislation. However, it is critical that those who are truly needy be helped. Children, the elderly, and the dysfunctional should be supported. What I object to is the culture of overdependence by those who have never developed their innate skills and the capacity to be independent.

When I did my doctoral research in the Pruitt-Igoe housing project in St. Louis, if a child came home crying because another child had hit him or her, the mother invariably directed the child to go back outside and hit the kid back. "Don't allow anyone to beat you up unless you also defend yourself" was the standard refrain to sons and daughters alike. The children usually did as they were told, and they learned an important lesson in survival.

Self-defense, however, does not always mean that one has to commit bodily harm. It never means that one has to pick up a weapon. It may mean, instead, that one "gets even" by walking away from danger and devoting one's time to excelling as a student. It may mean using verbal skills, including humor. Survival skills are more often a subtle art than an audacious tit for tat.

"The can-do spirit," resilience, and survival or coping skills are essentially the same. Each of us has learned how to cope to varying degrees. How much is innate and how much is learned is diffi-cult to say. What is clear, however, is that resilience and coping skills can be taught. The can-do spirit is available to everyone. From the young to the old, the feeble to the strong, all of us have this power within us.

# 14

# The Ninth Lesson:
## *Stand Tall*

How do we define courage? How do we distinguish between courage and bravado? When I was a kid, courage meant having "nerve" or "guts" enough to take a stand, especially on matters of principle. It took courage to take an unpopular stance, stand up to attacks and criticism, defend one's views or beliefs, and persuade others to accept one's point of view. Bravado, on the other hand, meant being pompous, bombastic, and even cowardly when the deal went down.

Courage was one of the most fundamental things Mother taught us. Her father and mother had taught all their children to stand up for their rights no matter who was violating them. Mother's brothers told us stories about how they fought white boys their age if they called them out of their names. Papa, my maternal grandfather, preached to them daily that they were "as good as any white man."

"Do what's right, no matter who does wrong," Mother admonished. "If you don't have enough nerve to take a stand, whatever it is you believe in can't be that important." In her view, you weren't responsible for your birth, but you were responsible for what you became. Nobody wanted to associate with someone who had no backbone. Backbone was what it was all about. Backbone to take a stand. Backbone to search for who you were. Backbone to demand your dignity even under a harsh system of racial segregation and discrimination. Backbone to dare to have the same dreams and aspirations for your children that whites and middle-class blacks had for theirs.

Fear and timidity were the enemies of people who were trying to hold on to their self-respect and dignity. If you were plagued with fear, it was impossible to stand tall. Others quickly learned to push you around. They squeezed your dignity from your body, and they knocked you down each time you tried to stand up again. In a part of the country where black men could be lynched for "eyeball rape" (looking lasciviously at a white woman), courage was not that easy to come by. There was no way to stand up to white people if you couldn't look them in the eye. Mother mastered the art of doing so, and she required no less of us.

I was going on twelve in 1955—the summer that the fourteen-year-old Chicagoan Emmett Till came down to Money, Mississippi, on holiday. Money was a one-horse town in the Delta that wasn't even on the map. I had never heard of Money until I read an article in the *Hattiesburg American* about Emmett's disappearance. The radio began to announce stories about the FBIs involvement in the case. Then there were a lot of articles in the

*Hattiesburg American* about the search for the boy, who, as the story went, had whistled at a white woman.

I had heard a lot about the cotton plantations in the Delta. The grown folks talked about how bad things were for Negroes up in the North Mississippi Delta. Uncle Archie said the Negroes there lived in little shotgun houses that stretched as far as you could see. They said the white people lived in big, pretty houses like some of those on Main Street and Hardy Street uptown.

Lynching, as far as I knew, had always involved men, not boys. Boys were children, and children were supposed to be off-limits—or so we thought. After Emmett Till's lynching, we all felt vulnerable. If, for whistling at a grown white woman, white men would go after a fourteen-year-old boy, savagely beat him, tie a cotton-gin fan around his neck, and hurl his dead body into a river, what wouldn't they do to me? It was no longer a matter of Daddy Bill and my uncles being vulnerable but me, too. Multiply me by thousands.

Dorie and I ran to the corner store every day at 4:30 P.M. to buy the newspaper. We kept the clippings of the lynching in a scrapbook and each day tearfully pored over the pictures and stories. Emmett Till was close to our age! We cried for him as if he were one of our brothers. When his body surfaced in the Tallahatchie River, we wondered, "How could they do that to him?" Dorie said that when she became a lawyer she'd fight to change things in the courts. And I said that I would help poor people get their rights so that when I became a social worker they wouldn't have to live under such terrible conditions.

We kids dramatized our idealized versions of how we hoped life would one day be for black people. Dorie, ever the imaginative one, set up a wood crate in the backyard and pretended to be the "Negro" lawyer arguing her cases for "Negro rights" before me, the judge. Of course, I always ruled in favor of blacks seeking their civil rights.

Many years later, when we were students at Tougaloo College, Dorie and I sat through the trial in the Jackson, Mississippi, courthouse of Byron de la Beckwith, who had murdered our mentor, the civil rights leader Medgar Evers. There was a parade of whites to the courtroom each day, including a visit, one day, from Governor Ross Barnett, who came to wish Beckwith well. Beckwith was not convicted for Medgar's murder until 1994, when Medgar's widow, Myrlie Evers Williams, was successful in getting a new trial. As I sat in the courtroom watching Beckwith being congratulated for murdering Medgar and being given the best wishes of the governor of the state, my mind raced back to those days in our backyard when we were children, playacting the courtroom scene we hoped would be carried out when Emmett Till's killers came to trial. I always felt that I would see the day when a white racist was convicted for killing a black man. And I did.

We were always encouraged in our dreams of justice for Emmett Till by our dear friend Dr. McLeod, who urged us on. Each week he ritually brought us his copies of the *Pittsburgh Courier*, the *Chicago Defender*, and *Jet* magazine so that we could read what the outside world was saying about the lynching. Dorie wrote a lengthy letter to the *Pittsburgh Courier* on her reactions to Emmett Till's lynching. She described how frightened she was as a fourteen-year-old growing up in such a hostile, brutal atmosphere. Mother was terrified that if the letter was published, the Ku Klux Klan might see it and retaliate by burning down our house. Although we eagerly looked for the letter in each week's paper, we were very disappointed; it was never published.

Then, in 1958, when I was fifteen years old, Mack Charles Parker, a black man, was lynched in the small town of Poplarville, Mississippi, for allegedly raping a white woman from Hattiesburg. While being held in the Pearl River county jail, a stone's throw from Hattiesburg, he was dragged down the concrete steps by a white mob. His body eventually turned up in the Pearl River.

This lynching shocked us. We hadn't expected it. His trial was coming up soon, and the rumor in Hattiesburg's black community was that his NAACP-hired lawyer (one of the three black attorneys in the state at the time), R. Jess Brown, would prove his innocence. Brown had evidence, we heard, that Mack Charles Parker had been somewhere else at the time of the alleged rape, and the truth was that the white woman hadn't been raped at all. I don't know if the rumors that circulated in Palmers Crossing were true, but one of them was that the white woman had had a rendezvous with her boyfriend. When she was pressed by her husband to reveal her whereabouts, she told him she had been raped. The black folks who lived in Palmers took this rumor as the gospel. Parker, we thought, had fallen innocent victim to her false claims, since he (and probably a thousand other black men in Poplarville) fit the general description of the alleged rapist: a black man.

After the lynching, Dorie and I rode the city bus downtown every day to overhear the conversations of the national and foreign press that converged on Hattiesburg to cover the event. We reasoned that these "outsiders" (the press) were our friends, because, unlike the local whites, they didn't believe in segregation. Even their accents were different from those of all the white people we knew. When Mack Charles Parker's body surfaced in the river, we cried. We cried for him and for his family; we also cried for our father and our brothers. If they could do that to him, and he wasn't guilty, we thought they could just as easily murder any of the black men in our family. I don't remember any other time when I was more frightened. Yet I was never more determined that one day things would be different. I suppose that for the first time I understood why my mother was so protective of my brothers.

My younger brother, Fred, was about thirteen years old at the time. Even though he was still a young boy, Mother drew him closer into her protective web, not allowing him to stray for more than a few minutes at a time up to Hudson's grocery store, where he worked on Saturdays bagging groceries. "Fred, don't hang around up there in the Crossing," she'd say. "You know what they did to that Parker boy." Mother admonished Fred to "mind your own business," which meant that he was to keep to himself, not get too friendly with the whites, especially the women, and hurry home as quickly as possible. Being courageous didn't mean that you had to take foolish chances.

Mother and Daddy Bill rarely discussed racial issues openly. Having grown up under severe oppression, they had learned early in their lives how to survive. Their strategy was to keep a low profile with whites. While they despised "Uncle Toms," they would never have joined the NAACP in the 1950s and early 1960s. In their own subdued way, however, they frequently "got white people told," which was Mother's way of saying she told them not to disrespect her and they never repeated the offense. Of course, they chose their battles carefully. Daddy Bill walked off his job many times when his white supervisor treated him in a racist manner. He came home for lunch every day, and once in a while he would still be there when we kids got home from school.

"Why is Daddy Bill at home?" I asked Mother.

"That white man who supervises him said something nasty to him, so he just walked off the job and came home," she explained. "There is no reason for him to talk bad to Bill. He's working as hard as he can."

He never told us the details, and we children never

asked what happened. In the end, we knew that he went back only after the boss, Joe Morris, who owned Joe Morris Motors and was a fairly decent type, called our home, apologized for the supervisor's behavior, and asked him to return to work. Though he was totally dependent upon his job to support his family, Daddy Bill was determined to maintain his dignity and his pride. "Don't ever let anyone take your pride from you," he always admonished us. "It's the most valuable thing you have."

Mother, too, insisted that we stand tall. "Don't let anybody push you around," she often said. "Don't let anyone walk over you." Indeed, we learned by example.

The risks she taught us to take became easier as our faith in God increased. The adults taught us that God would protect us if we stood tall, as long as we didn't display a wanton disregard for danger. "Lay your burdens at the feet of Jesus," the ministers preached on Sunday mornings. "If you have the courage of your convictions, then he will make your burdens easy, and lighten your heavy load." When I joined the civil rights movement in college, the theory and practice of nonviolence resonated with my childhood teachings about the protection God would provide if your cause was a just one.

I cannot say that Dorie and I had a vast amount of courage as children. Perhaps no more or less than my peers. However, we were always reaching for the sky because it was expected of us, as if it were a birthright. As a consequence, I learned fairly early in life that courage did not necessarily mean the absence of fear. Courage meant that you were or could be a risktaker. During the civil rights movement there were times when I was scared to death, but I was never too frightened to stop participating. The risks were well worth taking, I decided. I would have to learn to manage my fear in other ways.

*"Standing tall" means having the courage to stand by your beliefs, even if other people disagree—and even if you are afraid. People today live with all kinds of fears—fears that I call their "little demons." These little demons can virtually shut your system down, to the point where you become dysfunctional.*

*Some adults are afraid to "step on the ice" for fear that they will go down. What they really fear is hidden someplace in their minds. They have fears and phobias they never came to terms with when they were children. Now, as adults, they are trapped in the daily monotony that they feel is a safe refuge. But it is anything but safe. It actually stifles and cripples until they are neither capable of realizing their own full potential nor of helping their children to become all they are capable of being. You'll never know what the ice feels like if you don't try to skate on it.*

# 15

# The Tenth Lesson:

## *Your Word*
## *Is Your Bond*

Integrity is the firm adherence to your entire system of values. People of integrity stand by their moral code, and they are incorruptible.

One shining example of integrity is Muhammad Ali, the world's best-known athlete. I recently came across some words he spoke in 1968, when he was the center of controversy because he refused to be drafted into the military. He had joined the Nation of Islam, and had changed his slave name, as he called it, from Cassius Clay to Muhammad Ali. For these actions, he was severely attacked. Although he was the undisputed heavyweight champion of the world, boxing officialdom refused to allow him to retain his title or to fight. Because Ali was a young black man who had achieved so much, most African Americans admired his integrity and his deeply held convictions. He was unusual in the strength of his convictions and his belief that it would have been dishonest of him to join the military.

At that soul-trying time, Ali said, "I could make millions if I led my people the wrong way, to something I know is wrong. So now I have to make a decision. Step into a billion dollars and denounce my people or step into poverty and teach them the truth. Damn the money. Damn the heavyweight championship. I will die before I sell out my people for the white man's money. The wealth of America and the friendship of all the people who support the war would be nothing if I'm not content internally and if I'm not in accord with the will of Almighty Allah."

African American history is full of stories about the Alis who made the decision that to be able to live with themselves is the most important thing of all. Their personal sense of integrity was far more important than all the riches the world could offer. All the money in the world could not have sufficed for Ali, Nat Turner, Harriet Tubman, Fannie Lou Hamer, Ella Baker, Ida B. Wells, and countless others like them.

As time passes, there are fewer and fewer such individuals. People who gain national prominence rarely stand up for inconveniently principled positions, nor are they willing to pay the price for having these views. Watergate remains the national symbol of lying, stealing, and dishonor at the highest level of government in the free world. Today, children can see government officials going on trial for their misdeeds. They may know someone who steals and hustles for a living—who gets up each morning to go out and "rip off" hard-working, honest people. Most kids see examples of greedy, immoral behavior in the entertainment and news media every day.

But we need to remember that before today's population explosion of professional scam artists and spinmeisters, the truth was the truth and a lie was a lie. Children were taught the difference. Dishonor came to those who lied, while acceptance in the group was held out to those who told the truth.

Integrity was once as common as a handshake. With a handshake, people in the old communities sealed deals and made commitments that carried heavy responsibilities and consequences. They could do this because they trusted each other's integrity. They believed that the person they were doing business with was morally upright, responsible, and dependable. This trust was not a one-shot deal, nor was it easily extended. People knew each other well, they knew the family, and they knew what kind of person you were based not only on your behavior but on your lineage. They knew how you had been raised. They knew whether you were a person of character.

A dear friend, Al Martins, whose father came to America from the Cape Verde Islands, said that his father used an African proverb to teach him about character-building. His father used to say that the measure of a man is "the stone on his head." What he meant was that long before you die, people will draw their conclusions about the way you have lived. Your epitaph is written as you go through life. This stone is on your head already. When you die, this measure, not the headstone on your grave, will be your legacy.

Mother expressed the same idea a little differently. She used to say that you don't have to worry about what others say or think about you because all your critics have to do is look at your children and how they behave, and your children's children as well.

Some people are known for what they do, some are known for what they say, but few are known for who they are. Among the latter is the great educator Mary

McLeod Bethune. Toward the end of her life, this remarkable leader took the time to write down her legacy. "If I have a legacy to leave my people," she wrote, "it is my philosophy of living and serving. As I face tomorrow, I am content. I think I have spent my life well. I pray now that my philosophy may be helpful." Although her life spoke for itself, her legacy offers a definitive lesson in the integrity that is such an essential part of the system of African American values:

Sometimes I ask myself if I have any other legacy to leave. Truly my worldly possessions are few. Yet, my experiences have been rich. From them I have distilled principles and policies in which I believe firmly, for they represent the meaning of my life's work. They are the product of much sweat and sorrow. Perhaps in them is something of value. Here, then, is my legacy.

I leave you LOVE. Love builds. It is positive and hopeful. It is more beneficial than hate. Love thy neighbor is a precept which could transform the world if it were universally practiced.

I leave you with HOPE. Yesterday our ancestors endured degradation, yet they retained their dignity. Today, we direct our economic and political strength toward winning a more abundant and secure life.

I leave you A THIRST FOR KNOWLEDGE. Knowledge is the prime need of the hour. More and more, we are taking full advantage of hard-won opportunities for learning. If we continue in this trend, we will be able to rear increasing numbers of strong, purposeful men and women equipped with vision, mental clarity, health and education.

I leave you THE CHALLENGE OF DEVELOPING CONFIDENCE IN ONE ANOTHER. We must spread out as fast and as far as we can, but we must also help each other as we go.

I leave you A RESPECT FOR THE USE OF POWER. We live in a world which respects power above all things. Power, intelligently directed, can lead to more freedom. It has always been my first concern that power should be placed on the side of human justice. We must select leaders who are wise and courageous, and of great moral stature and ability. We have great leaders among us today. We have had other great men and women of the past: Harriet Tubman, Sojourner Truth, and Mary Church Terrell.

I leave you FAITH. Without faith nothing is possible. With it, nothing is impossible. Faith in God is the greatest power, but great too is faith in oneself.

I leave you RACIAL DIGNITY. I want us to maintain our human dignity at all costs. We must recognize that we are the custodians as well as the heirs of a great civilization. We have given something to the world and for this we are proud and fully conscious of our place in the total picture of mankind's development. Despite many crushing burdens and handicaps, I have risen from the cotton fields of South Carolina to found a college, administer it during its years of growth, become a public servant in the government and country, and a leader of women.

I leave you A DESIRE TO LIVE HARMONIOUSLY WITH YOUR NEIGHBOR. I leave you, finally, A RESPONSIBILITY TO OUR YOUNG PEOPLE. We have a powerful potential in our youth and we must have the courage to change old ideas and practices so that we may direct their power toward good ends.

*"Your word is your bond" means that you can be trusted because your values are incorruptible. You live by your code, confident that no matter what comes, your integrity is complete. You can be honest and content. Living according to only some of your values is not enough to ensure a reputation for integrity. Teaching only some of your values is not enough to give your children a legacy of integrity. Integrity requires living with all your values intact.*

# PERSONAL
## TRANSITIONS—
## THE POWER OF
## INTIMATE TIES

# 16

# Saving Our Relationships

I was twenty-nine years old when I got married. I remained married for eleven years, but I have been divorced longer than I was married. I always expected to remain married "until death do us part." Divorce was an enemy of stable and enduring families, I surmised, hence my decision to "stick it out no matter what." Moreover, three of my four sisters had married and divorced. I was determined that I would not share their fate. At least one of us had to hold up the banner for having a marriage that had survived the odds.

Several things honed my attitude toward marriage. My mother and father were divorced when I was about two years old, and soon after that she married Daddy Bill. One of Mother's favorite homilies was: "The first man you marry may not be your husband." By that she meant that it was possible to make a mistake in selecting a spouse, and divorce was acceptable under these conditions. But what was important was that you be able to recognize the right qualities in a mate the next time around. Still, I decided to prove the oddsmakers wrong, because I wanted to show everyone, including Mother, that I could make the right choice the first time around. Indeed, I wanted to prove that the first man I married would be my husband.

I also believed (and still do) firmly and unequivocally in the institution of marriage. Above and beyond being in love and compatible with my chosen mate, I revered the institution itself. I considered divorce to be a failure of my own personal expectations as well as a matter of failing my race. I had done research on black families and written so much in defense of black male-female relationships. When white sociologists referred to the "deterioration of the black family," I was outraged. How dare they use such off-putting language to describe relationships that had endured so much hardship in the past but had still survived? I asked. In effect, I had come to believe that the way to prove these sociologists wrong, in part, was to show that I could have a lasting relationship. But real life doesn't work that way.

After much anguish, I realized that my personal relationship had little or nothing to do with my beliefs in the institution of marriage. Each relationship has its own inner reality, and no amount of ideology or scholarly debate changes this fundamental fact. Thus after eleven years of marriage and one child—including several very satisfying years—and with much regret, I decided to call it quits. I accepted the reality of divorce without feeling that I was a personal failure.

My greatest concern was how to maintain my ten-year-old son's stability and give him as nurturing and secure an environment as I possibly could. I was determined that our son would not suffer unnecessarily the ill effects of the divorce. I had been the child of a divorce, and I remembered all too well how difficult it is for a child to cope with feelings of having been rejected by one parent, even if that isn't the case. I was also determined that my ex-husband and I would work hard to have a civil relationship with each other, because it would certainly help our son to adjust to the divorce. Perhaps it was for these reasons that, in part, my faith in the institution of marriage did not waver.

I still believe that marriage is the best and the most effective way to provide personal satisfaction as well as a stable foundation for our children, our communities, and the survival of our people. After all, slaves who didn't have the right to marry legally nevertheless found ways to form stable and enduring common-law marriages. They realized that their own survival was interwoven with the degree to which they could develop and sustain this most basic and important relationship between a man and a woman.

Slaves, therefore, gave their family names to their children and pledged fidelity to each other. This legacy was carried on in my family among my grandparents and parents, as well as my aunts, uncles, and cousins, many of whom had long-lasting marriages. My mother's old saying about finding the right mate the second time around was true for her, because she and Daddy Bill had been married for forty-nine years when she died.

This most enduring of relationships remained in force for many generations. It was not until the 1960s that we began to see large numbers of black marriages come unraveled. In 1950, 78 percent of black families had two parents; by 1960, the rate had declined only slightly, to 74 percent. But those rates continued to spiral chaotically out of control throughout the 1970s and 1980s to the present. In 1997, only 46 percent of black families were married-couple families. The consequences of these conditions are far-reaching.

What happened to our marriages? What are the consequences of our failed relationships, and how can we get back on track? Many of these changes in our marriages have come about as a result of economic conditions, the changing roles of women, and so forth. The entry of women into the workforce gave us the freedom to become more economically independent. With this independence, women were freed from the traditional roles of homemaker and mother. Economic empowerment allowed many women to become more self-reliant, and to have a broader number of options than ever before.

One of the options women had was the right to decide when, and indeed whether, they would marry and have a traditional family life. As an increasing number of black women went to college, their options expanded significantly. The traditional roles they had carried out were suddenly being challenged as passé or dysfunctional. The traditional perceptions we have had of the strong black woman who sits at the apex of a matriarchal society became an anachronism for many. The relative freedom women now have has militated against their traditional role as the self-sacrificing head of household who keeps the family together no matter what.

Economic independence allowed women to postpone marriage, to move out on their own, and to have an equal say in the household finances, because they were also wage earners. This new independence has been a double-edged sword. It increased the family's income, and it gave women more opportunities to develop their potential outside the home, but it also disrupted the stability of family life. Working mothers no longer have enough time to do many of the duties that were traditionally carried out by women. The added stresses and strains of trying to manage and juggle all the things women have to do have also caused disruption in the relations between men and women.

Today, more and more women are choosing to go it alone if being married also means having a mate who does not pull his own weight. We are less likely to embrace the role of the self-sacrificing "queen mother" of our forebears, and to go it alone. Black women are also less likely to stay in unhappy relationships, including marriages, solely because traditional values dictate that they should. But there are those who would argue that we are too quick to opt for divorce as the solution to an incompatible marriage.

The stick-to-it-iveness that our ancestors had is becoming a distant memory. In fact, some of my friends look back on their own relatives' marriages and vow never to make the sacrifices their grandmothers, mothers, and aunts made. The movement for sexual equality has had a strong influence on black women, despite notions to the contrary. Black women have not been insulated from the changes that have taken place in society at large.

My generation is one that is caught between the world of our mothers and fathers and that of our sons and daughters. We are the transitional generation that is still trying to find our place, since we are at the midpoint between modernity and postmodernism. Our children have been the direct beneficiaries of the vast changes in sex roles that have swept across America. Our sons, no less than our daughters, have grown up at a very different time and in a very different place than we did. The sexual revolution that my generation experienced has been an accepted norm among our heirs.

The independence of women has also had a profound effect on male-female relations because women became less dependent than ever on their mates for economic survival. The introduction of contraceptive technology in the 1960s freed women as never before. No longer preoccupied with pregnancy, women who took control of their own sexuality were able to separate sexual involvement from the act of reproduction. In effect, women who came of age in the 1960s and 1970s were the first generation to benefit from the sexual revolution. The combination of more education and better job prospects allowed many women to postpone marriage and starting a family.

Obviously, there have been many changes in the lives of black men as well. The black man's indisputable role as the authority figure in the family has declined. With the decline in authority, men have also lost some of the prestige and power they once claimed in their relationships with black women. Men have also expanded their options to include non–African American women, which exacerbates the conflict. Black women are especially critical of black men who date and marry white women, because in their view this is "taking black men away from" black women.

The high rates of unemployment, school dropout, substance abuse, and incarceration among black men have done more than anything else to bring about the downward spiral in male-female relations. Without an adequate way to sustain a stable relationship, many black men have found themselves essentially "pushed out" of their traditional roles. I do not intend to assign blame to either the men or the women. I do, however, feel that, while each individual must assume personal responsibility for his or her actions, some of the blame must also be placed at the foot of the society that continues to practice one of the most heinous forms of racial and class discrimination against black men.

The poor in the underclass are the individuals who have experienced the greatest amount of personal and public dislocation in their lives. As a result of not being able to form and maintain a romantic attachment with a mate, many have been deprived of the caring and sharing that bring not only personal stability but a sense of familial and communal permanence. Today, we can find men and women across the urban landscape fighting the blight and the interminable insecurity that have produced the most profound form of alienation we have ever seen. The lack of attachment is all too apparent in the lives of the homeless men and women who populate the cities of this nation.

Each time I see homeless people, I wonder who they are and what journey has led them to this horrific lifestyle. It occurs to me that perhaps they were husbands and wives at one point in their lives. Perhaps they are mothers and fathers whose lives got out of control and they had few opportunities to pull themselves back before they reached the edge of despair.

Most of us do not live on the edge of despair. Our lives are more or less under our control, and we have made conscious decisions about our relationships. Looking back at my own life, I wonder whether it would have been more fulfilling if I had remained married. I never expected that I would be divorced as long as I have. I have many friends who are divorced—men and women who must have expected as I did that their divorced status would be but a brief interlude. However, one year turned into two, and two turned into four, until some of us looked up and discovered we had been divorced for a decade. And we had adapted! Adapted to being a single person. Adapted to a lifestyle that required that we fend for ourselves in the workplace, in the community, and on the home front. We got used to taking trips with our friends, with our children, or we went alone, and found that it wasn't such a bad thing. Among our friends were people who had never married at all. We discovered how to re-create family relationships as single men and women. Some of us are still holding out on making any commitments until we find another black partner, while others of us have begun to date people from other cultures and races.

In the meantime, we hope. We hope for more healing. We hope for the soothing balm and tenderness that allow us to see each other as whole men and women who should be building together rather than tearing ourselves apart. We hope for the sustained chatter that comes from two people who love to laugh together, play together, and love together. And we hope for the future.

> *Surely our children's relationships will have a better chance of working if they see healthy role models in their parents, aunts and uncles, grandparents and friends. Young people are not looking for problem-free relationships to model. They simply need to see couples working things out; struggling together rather than separately; and making up rather than separating and divorcing after a disagreement. When we can be models of love and courage, we will not only help our sons and daughters to sort out how to make relationships work, but we will find our own happiness.*

# 17

# Loving Our Children

Frantz Fanon, an Algerian psychiatrist, wrote that "each generation must define its mission, fulfill it, or betray it." For most young people today, this is more likely to be a difficult rather than an easy process. The entire landscape of adolescence has changed dramatically. While it was a fairly benign period thirty years ago, it is now filled with minefields for children of every economic class.

At best, the period of late adolescence and young adulthood is one of the most unstable and difficult periods of adjustment. Adolescents in American society typically use this time to sort out many of the lifelong issues, such as identity, values, attitudes, and behavior patterns, that confront them. Consciously and unconsciously, they must grapple not only with *what* but also with *whom* they wish to become. Oftentimes it is a subtle process, and the individual is not aware of what is taking place because he or she is not yet capable of deep introspection.

Even the thousands of parents who can provide their children with the space they need for this preparatory period of their lives are often caught in a web of danger. Parents can assure the safety and security of their children only to the extent that they can provide these things for themselves. We live in such dangerous times that we should consider all of our children and youths to be potentially at risk. Gone are the days when we could automatically regard only poor children as being at risk.

The experimentation that often accompanies this period can cause more severe consequences than ever before. Young people are testing limits and experimenting with various roles in an atmosphere of increasing danger. The danger of drugs, violence, and a plethora of other social problems threatens this generation in ways that no previous generation has experienced. Children must be understood in the context not only of their developmental cycle but also of the difficult environmental considerations in which so many of them live.

I have talked to countless adolescents about their experiences, and they readily discuss their anxieties and fears, and their feelings of depression and anger. One of the most memorable interviews I conducted was with a self-styled "street authority," who, despite the AK-47 he carried underneath his coat, admitted that he is very frightened when he walks down a particular street late at night. The gun did not relieve his normal and natural adolescent fears. He also said that he is more likely to shoot someone when he is in this type of situation than not.

The young killer can neither discover nor sustain a healthy concept of self under the conditions he places himself in. Fortunately, the majority of African American children have a good chance of navigating this period of their lives successfully with our help. The important thing to remember about loving and supporting your child now is that no matter how tough it is for you during this period, it is also very difficult for your adolescent. Even so, this is the time to imprint your mark. It is not the time to throw caution to the wind. With our help and prayers, young people do grow out of their difficult years.

Keeping my son alive long enough to see adulthood has been a mammoth task in and of itself, because he, like many other middle-class children, has grown up in the shadow of the ghetto. He has come of age in full view of police officers who assumed that because he was black and male, he must also be ready to commit a crime. I have lain awake many nights until I finally heard the key turn in the lock. Only then did I know that he was safe— until the next time he went out. I have vacillated between protecting him like a mother hen and allowing him to grow and mature into adulthood free and unfettered. It hasn't been easy.

Writing this book gave me an opportunity to try to understand how my son sees the world. My first meeting with baby Thomas was a good indication of how he would turn out. Today, he is friendly, animated, athletic, persuasive, and, at times, relentless in the pursuit of his goals, or in badgering me or anyone else about something that he wants to get done. He is now a senior in college.

Are there major things he intends to improve on when he has children? How does he envision the world and his place in it? Did I leave something of substance with him that will help him to grow up to be a strong, caring, conscientious, and honorable person? Have I earned the right to be called Mama Thomas, based on who he has become?

I hesitated to ask Thomas these questions directly,

153

because I feared that with his usual candor he would tell me that I had really blown it. Candor is difficult, because we all want to feel that we have been successful in this, the most important undertaking of our lives. So I asked one of his female friends to interview him for me, and he opened up a lot more to her than he did to me. Here is what he said:

"Mom has always been there for me even though I am a guy. She taught me to look before I leap. For example, she taught me to find out what a person is like as an individual before I get involved with them. I can go to my mother with any problem, even though I'm a guy. She also invested in my future by sending me to a safe place to get my education.

"Having established that fact, though, I can say that our relationship has gone through several stages. I have often gotten annoyed because my mom is overprotective. That is why we have gotten into all the fights we've had over the years. From the time I was fifteen or sixteen until I was about twenty-one, there was a lot of strain between us because she tried to hold me back. She was afraid of what might happen to me. She knew D.C. was a dangerous place for a young black man: It has the highest murder rate in the country. Mom didn't want me to get killed. After I turned twenty-one, we became best friends.

"I learned a lot through the things we did together as a family—like trips to the beach, vacations, riding our bikes, and hanging out with my friends."

After my husband, Walter, and I divorced, I became the custodial parent, even though Thomas spent each weekend with his dad. We had a flexible arrangement that allowed Thomas to spend time with Walter whenever either of them wanted him to do so. My view is that children need their fathers as much as they do their mothers. We made the decision that we would not allow our disagreements to have a negative influence on either parent's relationship with our child. He went on trips with each of us at different times. Somehow, it worked, and he learned other lessons along the way:

"Mom taught me how to treat women. She said I should treat them with respect, and that I should have respect for myself, too. She said that I couldn't have self-respect unless I treated women with respect. I also don't want to disrespect myself by getting into trouble with the police.

"What I think most about when I think of my mother is that she works so hard. She worked all the time when I was growing up. She used to take me to work with her when she was teaching at the university. I used to sit in the classroom and draw on the blackboard while she was teaching. Her students were nice to me. This familiarized me with college. My experience was totally opposite from the movie *Boyz 'n the Hood*.

"No matter how busy Mom was, she came to my games, and she was always there for me when I needed her. She was very busy, but she took time off to be with me. That's one of the things I'm going to do for my children.

"I don't think I'm the typical guy insofar as morals are concerned. Mom and Dad taught me to have high morals by respecting women and adults. Mom would punish me if she found out I had disrespected adults.

"I knew her rules, even though I didn't always go by them. One time she went out of town for the weekend. She had already told me I couldn't invite my friends over for a party while she was away. I went ahead and had a party anyway. Well, my Aunt Dorie came over unexpectedly and saw me giving this party. She said, 'You know your mom won't approve of this.'

"The next time Mom went out of town, about a year later, I gave a small party thinking she wouldn't find out about it. I thought I'd cleaned up, but Mom immediately went to the trash and found the bottles. I said, 'God, she knows me so well.' We talked about it. I knew I had done wrong. I told her I was sorry I had let her down, and I promised I'd never do it again."

Yes, Thomas is my child. The fruit rarely falls far from the tree, as the old folks used to say. Yet I feel that some fundamental things that go beyond the obvious differences in economic status and my relationship with his father are different for him than they were for me. Here is what I see:

Just as spirituals gave way to gospel music, the struggle-based values of my generation and those that preceded mine may actually be on the verge of being transformed into something that is a little different. Thomas knows who he is. He identifies strongly as a black man, but he has not had to experience as much racism in everyday life as I did. His racial awareness as well as the diversity in our society shapes his definition of self. I think our kids have begun to add to the survival values of previous generations that are based on racial oppression. They have had the advantage of learning how to live with diverse populations and, in many instances, with more diverse role models and a wider sense of their options.

My niece Yodit confirms that perspective. Her sense of what it means to be a part of her generation is different from mine. Amazingly, when I asked her how her generation of African Americans defined their most challenging problems, Yodit replied, "I cannot speak for my generation at all. People's lives are too varied." We look at the world through different eyes. Nevertheless, Yodit is thoughtful about being a black woman today. She says: "As a young black woman, what are my opportunities and expectations? You ask whether I think I've been adequately prepared to lead a productive life? My answer is, the sky is the limit. Unlike previous generations of black Americans, I have seen great accomplishment by black men and women. There are ample examples. In addition, I do not feel that my race is a burden. At least, it hasn't been so far. I feel that if I tried, I could do virtually anything. I feel that I have been prepared for life."

I disagree with a lot of the critics who feel that young people today do not share their parents' sense of identity with other African Americans. I think kids who have been taught the values related to identity, family, responsibility, and community are very committed to finding ways to bring about equity between the races and social classes. One of the ways in which they express themselves politically is through the music of their generation: rap.

Another way they express themselves politically is through service. I decided that, in the absence of poverty and overt racial discrimination in Thomas's life, it was up to me to create opportunities for him to experience the struggle for human dignity. I therefore encouraged him to organize a campaign in his middle school to collect canned goods for the homeless, and I helped his teachers arrange transportation for the children to take the food to the shelter so they could *see* what the conditions of homeless and hungry people are. On Thanksgiving, we went to the shelters to help dispense food, part of which we had cooked. He volunteered to do errands for the elderly people in the community when he was in high school. He tutored a high school student when he was in college. He organized his own soccer team in an inner-city elementary school in Washington, got me to buy their uniforms, and enrolled them in the same indoor soccer league that he had played in when he was their age.

When all is said and done, however, the extent to which we are able to help our children develop good values is up to them. The timeless values of my generation may be finding new expression in our children. The ways in which they adapt the values of kindness, honesty, respect, courage, dignity, self-reliance, personal responsibility for their actions, hard work, and the desire for an education depend on what they encounter and initiate during their own journey through life. Thomas and Yodit have given me reason to be hopeful for their generation.

I am more sanguine about Thomas's outcome than I would have been five or even three years ago. There were times—when he was between sixteen and twenty-one—which I call his "crazy period," when "what does Mom know about this?" was a constant refrain. He was rebellious for the heck of it. At times, he wanted to dismiss out of hand my guidance based on my being the "mother" instead of the "father." I have cried at night with worry about his insistence on being free to explore the world around him, because I know that it is full of a violence that can engulf young black men.

But with a lot of patience and a lot of prayer, Thomas and I got through the crazy period. I always knew that if I could keep him safe and alive he would eventually be all right. It is almost hard for me to remember the stress and strain between us, the "raging hormones" period that caused him to declare himself to be "a man!" at sixteen, as if this declaration alone changed the fundamental fact that he was still dependent on his father and me to take care of him. He was typical of all adolescents, who are constantly changing. Their lives can shift from stability to confusion within an instant.

No matter how low they fall, don't give up on them is the advice I gave myself and the advice my friends and I gave one another. We knew that we had to give them the support mixed with the strong doses of discipline they would need as they tried to navigate the minefields of being a teenager. The adolescent pressures we experienced now greet our children when they are preadolescents. The pressures to conform have also increased many times over. There are not enough countervailing positive forces to offset the negative media images and other misbehavior they are exposed to.

It is still up to us to change this. No one else is going to change the environment for your children but you. If you give up, why shouldn't others? It is therefore critical that you develop an open, honest relationship with them. Encourage them to discuss what's on their minds, no matter how offensive it may be. This can be done without compromising your authority. If you don't know what's on their minds, you cannot intercede before they get into trouble. Also, it's better for them to talk to you than to someone who might be a bad influence.

I always gave Thomas my guidance, even when it appeared that it was going unheeded. Thus I am always pleasantly surprised—and this occurs with greater frequency as he ages—that he behaves as he has been taught to behave. Young people will usually fall back on the good home training and solid values you have given them. It may not be when you want them to, but trust me: Your valuable lessons are not wasted. I have also tried to teach him the importance of discipline, hard work, and achievement. He seems determined to do his best in the uncertain world of acting. I had to learn to accept his decision, and to support him in his efforts to achieve what he has chosen.

I am pleased that he is getting less materialistic as he gets older. The desire to wear the brand-name jeans, jackets, and the like has given way to normalcy. The brand names no longer have the cachet they once had. I would like to think that he is learning that those were hollow and false values. Only time will tell.

*It is difficult for parents to understand fully the strong pressures their children are experiencing. It is natural that in the midst of a heated debate over, say, privileges, you cannot always stand back and look at the issues raised by your children in an objective way. It is personalized, for it is personal. But whenever possible, try to take a step back and remember that the pressures you experienced are tame by comparison with those they're encountering. Also, remember that you were once their age and you probably felt that none of the adults in your life understood you, either.*

# PASSING
## ON THE
### LEGACY

# 18

# Timeless Treasures
# for the Family

What all of us want for our children is that they grow up in environments where they feel safe and secure; where their basic needs and some of their wants are met; and where all children recognize the importance of studying hard. We also want them to feel that we have provided them with the wherewithal to become successful workers, mates, and parents. Underlying this bright picture of the future is our assumption that our children will have a lasting set of values to guide them as they grow.

Today, however, fewer and fewer parents spend enough time with their children to teach them values. The amount of time American parents spend with their children has dropped 40 percent during the past quarter century. Unless this trend is reversed, many of the timeless treasures you and I remember from our collective past will become irrelevant. Even our language reflects this worrisome trend. We talk about spending "quality" time with our kids instead of just plain old time. In some families, baby-sitters and teachers have replaced parents and grandparents as primary caregivers. In 1965, the average parents had roughly thirty hours of contact with their children each week. Today, according to the Family Research Council, this figure has fallen to seventeen hours. According to the Benton Foundation, when kids are asked how they would improve their families, they invariably say they wish there were more opportunities for fun time.

We should be making an extra effort to make sure that whatever time we have is well spent. First, take a personal assessment to determine that you are giving your children as much time as you possibly can, and using that time as wisely as possible. Use it to teach them your values in the following ways:

1. **Show that you believe a good reputation is critical.** "A good name is more desirable than riches," said the Bible. Help your children pick friends who have good character, and stay away from those who present problems. Show your concern about good and bad behavior.

2. **Treat authority figures with deference.** Respect teachers, the elderly, and other people who are entrusted with the job of helping your children. At the same time, also teach children to steer clear of adults who would harm them.

3. **Teach morality.** Do not hesitate to show that certain ideals and standards need to be upheld. Teach your children that everything is not relative. There is good behavior and there is bad behavior. They should uphold the good.

4. **Put your family first.** Priorities need to be reexamined and reordered. Cut out the unnecessary things from your schedule. Give your family greater priority than you give your job, club activities, and other commitments.

5. **Show that you believe money is not everything.** Balance spending more time with the family against earning more money. Decide which deserves the highest priority: a new pair of sneakers and jeans for your children or more time spent together as a family.

6. **Show that manners and grooming are important.** Being courteous, especially to adults, and having good manners and good grooming habits (neat clothing and combed hair) are basic to children's self-respect and to the respect they show to others.

7. **Minimize negative influences.** Steer your children away from influences that do not support your values. Seek out other families at church, school, and elsewhere who share your values.

8. **Make names special.** Tell your children the story of how their names were chosen and what these names mean. Was a particular name chosen to honor a relative, in recognition of a traditional African name, or because it is a beautiful sound?

9. **Make a family album for each child.** A personal album helps to reinforce a child's sense of personal importance and personal history/ biography.

10. **Celebrate the major milestones in your family.** Celebrate all of the family's achievements (a

new job, good grades, a good report card, birthdays, and the anniversary of your marriage).

11. **Carry on family traditions and create new ones.** Practice traditions from your own childhood, and find ways to deviate from regular life to create new family rituals. These events create a sense of cohesion that binds the family together. The rituals can be organized around holidays (an annual Easter egg hunt in your backyard, a special treat for achievement) or on the spur of the moment.

12. **Perform a family play.** For special occasions such as birthdays, Christmas, and the like, the family can write a play together or use a script from the local library. This gives the family something positive to share, and it teaches children how to build self-confidence by expressing themselves. My son's godparents have performed a Christmas pageant for twenty-five consecutive holidays, with all family members and friends participating.

13. **Plan a family reunion.** Find things for everyone in the family to do for the celebration, such as assembling the mailing list, choosing a site (take the children with you to visit the sites under consideration if possible), selecting the reunion colors, designing the T-shirts, choosing games for the cousins who will attend.

14. **Teach black history.** This should be done all year, but highlighted during Black History Month. Storytelling based on the parents' and grandparents' lives is a good starting point. Reading books on the lives of famous black people inspires high self-esteem.

15. **Envision a future.** Children must be able to see themselves as successful adults with careers in order to envision a future. Point out to them what their teachers, pediatrician, and dentist do in order to make these professions real to them. Reinforce their aspirations and goals whenever possible.

16. **Teach the can-do spirit.** Like courage, resilience is learned; it is not innate. Persistence produces success, not failure. If your children falter in their efforts to do something, be their cheerleader as they pick themselves up and try again until the task is accomplished.

17. **Draw a family tree.** Have your children interview their grandparents and other older relatives. This will give them a better sense of where they fit within the family. Also, tell children stories about your life and encourage them to tell you stories about theirs.

18. **Teach how to solve problems.** Give children tasks to perform that involve figuring out how to get the job done. It can be organizing their toys in the toy chest or helping to plan the family's vacation schedule.

19. **Recognize family heroes and "sheroes."** Make up bedtime stories using anecdotes about relatives, especially stories that exemplify courage, achievement, and sacrifice.

20. **Expose children to the world.** At first glance, this might seem difficult. But the world is at their fingertips via the Internet, the Discovery Channel, *National Geographic*, free museums, educational films, and through reading. Take

your children to the library to check out books, and to storytelling hours at the library and at children's bookstores.

21. **Limit television.** Control the media influences in your home by limiting TV to certain hours and certain days.

22. **Establish family time.** In putting your family first, declare firmly that you are going to build family time into your schedule. The family time has to be valued as "sacred" and should not be infringed on by anything short of a crisis. Each issue that confronts you has to be measured in terms of what it will take away from your family. This includes working overtime and taking on extra obligations that aren't as important as the family.

23. **Make your home part of a learning network.** Everyone in the family should be a reader. Children model their behavior on that of their parents. It is not accidental that many adults who are voracious readers had parents who were readers. Similarly, the entire family needs to learn to surf the Internet, to acquire reference materials, and to play games that have an educational purpose. This allows learning skills to be woven into everyday life.

24. **Minimize the media's commercial impact in your home.** Parents must use their habits as consumers and shoppers to help them make this determination.

25. **Give children lots of hugs.** Children who are hugged by you are less likely to turn to boyfriends and girlfriends to get that much-needed physical expression of affection.

26. **Buy a pet.** When children say they need someone to love and call their own, a pet is often just the right answer.

27. **Encourage volunteering.** Teenage girls can volunteer as Candy Stripers in the nurseries of their local hospital or at day-care centers. Boys can tutor or coach. It's better than becoming a teen parent, and it's good training for becoming parents later.

28. **Teach the "old-fashioned" values as long as you live.** Children need to know what these values—respect, reputation, and responsibility—mean to you as an adult. They also need to know that these values are forever. Don't stop giving your children guidance and advice simply because they have reached adulthood. They will still need your parenting. Do not allow the personal antagonism between you and your ex-spouse to come between you and your children. Try to stay involved with your children for as long as you live.

29. **Build a large support system.** If you don't have an extended family nearby, recruit friends, neighbors, church members, and your co-workers.

30. **Seek role models for yourself.** Parents, especially if they are single, often need people to whom they can turn for advice, support, and, occasionally, consolation. An older neighbor, a co-worker, or a church member can give you the adult parenting support you need. They can also be a substitute for the grandfather or grandmother your children do not have.

31. **Teach self-sufficiency.** There is no better way for children to recognize and appreciate their own inner source of power. A young man or woman who is self-sufficient will not have to rely on welfare or on you. Self-sufficiency is the greatest gift you can give your children. It will pay off forever.

32. **Emphasize marketable skills.** Keep your children in school long enough to get the skilled training they will need to become economically self-sufficient, whether it is college, trade school, or some other type of training.

33. **Teach how to make wise choices.** Teach children to be independent-minded and self-critical so they can make the best choices possible.

34. **Teach your children about their sexuality.** Counsel them on abstinence. By understanding the potential consequences of premature sexual involvement, children learn that their bodies belong to them. They should not feel that they must have sexual relations in order to "please someone" or to "prove a point." They should treat their bodies as sacred. Sexual activity needs to be postponed until they are emotionally mature and financially independent.

35. **Model courage.** Teach your children that courage is not necessarily the absence of fear, because fear is a normal part of our lives. It is the ability to take a stand, especially on a principle, when necessary. Children will be pressured to go along with the crowd in order to be accepted. You and others—educators, counselors, ministers—need to create sanctuaries of

safe options that children can turn to so that it becomes easier for them to resist the temptations of negative behavior.

36. **Reward extraordinary courage.** Establish "model of courage" prizes in your churches, communities, and schools for children who do brave things, including taking a stand on behalf of what's right.

37. **Practice the simple art of always telling the truth.** Do not deviate from this standard. The most important thing is to be consistent. If your children don't hear you tell lies, they're not likely to do so, either. Let your children know that you are pleased with their honesty. Remember, they need reinforcement, but do not treat honesty as if it were an unusual act. Kids need to view honesty as the normal way people behave.

# 19

# Timeless Treasures for the School and the Community

Each of us is a member of a community, but our communities cover a broad landscape. These days, your community is where you find it. It may consist not only of family but also of friends, neighbors, and people who live across town and in other cities. You can build your community with the people who live in your apartment building or on your cul-de-sac. We graft our communities together out of the scraps of whole cloth we find, and weave them together like a beautiful tapestry by phone, fax, e-mail, and occasional face-to-face visits.

We measure our communities by the quality of our institutions, and for our children's sake the schools should be the most important of these. When our communities are working, our institutions can be relied on to assist, give support, and reinforce our priorities and values. Good schools and strong institutions thrive on traditional values. Wherever communities have broken down, we urgently need to put our values in action, especially in the urban areas where anonymity has taken over.

Rebuilding requires more than individual effort. The entire environment must be engaged—the local institutions, civic leadership, businesses, labor, educators, churches, foundations, as well as individuals. If we are serious about making a difference, cooperative efforts should pervade our plans and actions. Self-sufficiency and empowerment as individuals and as a group should be our goal. Government grants are no substitute for the sustained strength people find in shared interests and goals. Success will come when we assume leadership in building our communities, especially schools that are good for our children and are in keeping with our values. Here are some methods that will help you to focus your community and schools on our highest values:

1. **Offer incentives to teachers, police officers, firefighters, and others to move to the neighborhoods in which they work.** Role models are most effective when children are exposed to them in natural, day-to-day ways. Professionals also become more invested in what goes on in communities when they are residents.

2. **Offer young black professionals incentives to become urban pioneers.** Housing tax credits and other rebates will encourage young professionals to move into rehabilitated housing in old neighborhoods. They can help to rebuild the schools, organize neighborhood patrols, look out for the kids and the elderly on their block,

and receive the same in return from the old-timers. They will be easier to recruit before they have children.

3. **Organize parenting classes for adults.** Many adults who have successfully raised their own children have much to offer as teachers to new parents.

4. **Organize conflict-resolution classes.** These should be mandatory in all the homes, schools, churches, recreation centers, and other institutions that deal with young people. They need to be able to express their feelings, including their frustrations, to adults who are not only non-judgmental but will also direct them in a positive way.

5. **Form nonprofit organizations to develop partnerships with banks and other commercial institutions.** The lending institutions can work with community-development organizations to rehabilitate housing for teachers, police officers, firefighters, the clergy, recreation and youth workers, and others. This is good for business, too, because a stabilized neighborhood builds good customers.

6. **Organize retired men and women to be surrogate parents of young adults and grandparents to their children.** These elders can be jack-of-all-trade mentors to parents and children who have no one to fill this important role in their lives. Just as some elders teach parenting skills, they can also teach how to be effective community participants—leaders and followers. (This is a skill that has to be taught; it is not instinctive.)

7. **Establish a national black grandparents' registry through your local institutions.** Volunteers enlisted in every community can be surrogate grandparents to children who need them.

8. **Teach children to value, and not scorn, academic achievement.** The highest priority must be given to showing them how they can succeed through education. Many of the youths who tease their high-achieving peers and accuse them of trying to "act white" do not envision themselves with successful futures. Our job is to show them the concrete opportunities that are available to them.

9. **Clean up neighborhoods.** Good schools go hand in glove with decent housing and neighborhood pride.

10. **Insist that your schools teach today's survival skills.** Critical thinking, written and oral communication, and methods of information retrieval and computation are basic tools today.

11. **Teach self-esteem.** A basic, strong education must also give children a sense of purpose, the ability to envision a future as successful people, goals, a strengthened identity, and a measure of dignity for themselves and their peers.

12. **Educate the whole child.** Some children who perform at a high intellectual level may have acute personal needs, and vice versa. We cannot separate the child into different parts, as if we were dealing with an inanimate object. We want the whole person to be healthy.

13. **Send children to school every school day.** Challenge your children to see if they can maintain perfect attendance. Give them ribbons, certificates, and other incentives for trying to reach this milestone. This will help them to develop the habits of promptness, fortitude, and goal-setting.

14. **Establish community-school partnerships.** Children will be more effective if their parents, other caring adults, and teachers have a good working relationship. Help out at school. Volunteer in the classroom or raise money and seek out good equipment. Become an advocate for a child who does not have one.

15. **Teach the value of hard work as well as techniques for getting and keeping a job.** Schools should develop curricula that teach the importance of hard work. The courses should be taught in the schools, community centers, continuing-education programs, churches, and other civic organizations. This is a critical element in rebuilding values because a large number of young adults (many of whom are household heads) have never had jobs. They have subsisted on welfare, food stamps, and Section 8 housing vouchers. They cannot teach their children what they themselves do not know. They do not know how to conduct themselves in a job interview because they have never had that experience. A curriculum on the value and meaning of work should include heavy doses of the role that work has played in the history of black people, because by learning this history young people can develop pride and a sense of kinship with their

forebears. Not only do they need to learn to value their ability to earn a living but they also need the structure and order that work imposes on their lives. A habitual set of activities can be very meaningful in moving children toward a productive lifestyle.

16. **Intervene early to prevent a major problem.** The key time to influence youths is before puberty. Coming under the influence of the wrong crowd, using alcohol and drugs, breaking curfew, getting pregnant or impregnating someone are all examples of the kind of behavior that we should preempt.

17. **Support violence-prevention programs.** Parents, schools, churches, recreation centers, and other institutions and individuals have organized all-points intervention programs on violence reduction. We must teach all young people how to handle conflict and stress without resorting to violence.

18. **Enlist the young leaders in your community as peer counselors.** They are still young enough to understand what kids are going through. They can get inside the heads of their peers and give them advice.

19. **Start or join a role-model program.** There can never be too many role-model programs. The best role models are the ones that are in the family—the mothers and fathers, grandparents, aunts, and uncles with whom children interact on a regular basis. More fathers need to be shamed into accepting their responsibilities. Ditto for mothers. We also need role models from and for the middle class. Led by

groups like sororities, fraternities, professional organizations, and the like, many middle-class black organizations and their members have taken low-income children under their wings. The Concerned Black Men in Washington, D.C., has an outstanding record of achievement in mentoring young boys whose fathers are absent. Middle-class children can also benefit from these programs; some of them have absent fathers, too.

20. **Keep the schools open.**   Schools are community centers. They should be open for after-school activities, including supervised homework, recreation, and midnight basketball and other athletic programs. Adult education classes and community forums should be part of the ongoing activities. Schools can become the urban sanctuaries for our children.

# 20

# Timeless Treasures for the Church

The church has three roles: to anchor us spiritually, to inspire us, and to advocate a social gospel to help those who are least able to help themselves. While I recognize that some African Americans have left Christianity and adopted Islam, Buddhism, and other religions, my view is that whatever your religious beliefs are, they can help make stronger people, families, and communities. Regardless of your religion, I will refer to the physical place of worship and communion as the church.

Churches are the moral compass in teaching adults and youths alike the dos and don'ts that make up our traditional culture. To teach religion, morals, and ethics today, the church must find new ways to give the same timeless message of hope and inspiration it has provided for ages. While the medium of communication may have changed, the need to hear the message has not. We are still our brothers' and our sisters' keepers.

That means the church needs to begin to deal honestly and openly with social issues such as AIDS, homosexuality, and teen pregnancy. It can ill afford to refuse to approach these problems realistically. Families are desperate for progressive leadership, and the church can be a leader.

The church has always been the institution that embraces us all, stretching its arms to enfold us in the mercy, compassion, and sanctuary that give us comfort in times of need, and bring solace when we are down and out. Our churches have the historical right to reclaim the role of being the singular moral authority on issues of great importance. They must also be the institutions that motivate us to want to become better people, and to look beyond the dark clouds for the bright sunshine that awaits us.

How do we help our children to connect with the church, which for them may be an unknown element that we have too often ignored? How do we encourage them to appreciate the anchor that is available to them? We do so by stressing the "stuff" of our religious culture—the prayers and the scriptures, the hymns, gospels, and spirituals, the testimonies of faith and the ability to ask for forgiveness for the wrongs we have committed against each other. We start by teaching our toddlers the Bible verses, the catechism or Sunday School, the rituals of Sunday-morning service, or Mass. We take the willing young to confirmation classes and make sure they get the religious education they need to give them a body of doctrine in which to anchor their faith.

Here are some other ways in which we can introduce children to our religious traditions:

1. **Teach the Ten Commandments and the Golden Rule:** "Do unto others as you would have them do unto you." Reward your children for memorizing the Ten Commandments and the Golden Rule. Also, have them give you examples of what they mean when they say, "Thou shall not steal." Remember that the objective of the exercise is to enable them to apply these virtues to their own lives.

2. **Teach your favorite religious songs.** They may be spirituals, hymns, or gospels. If you are not Christian, teach your children the music of your faith. Remember that the idea is to recapture the songs so they can become a part of your children's lives. Then they can experience the beauty of the lyrics of "Precious Lord," as Mahalia Jackson sang it, or "To God Give the Glory," or the anthem "A Mighty Fortress Is Our God." The songs you cherished are the ones you should feel free to pass on. Each church has its own traditions, its own preferences, as well as collective traditions. Find your place in one of these churches. Make sure that your children can sing those songs, or hum along, as they hear them being sung in concert halls or on recordings.

3. **Return to the church, mosque, or temple as a family.** Children need to grow up with respect for a higher power that they can call on in times of need. Religion can also help to connect them with the belief systems of their ancestors, and allow them to frame their own morals and ethics.

4. **Sponsor children-friendly forums at your church on social issues.** A children-friendly setting allows young people to express themselves on these issues. Ask them to suggest topics that are of concern. Give them opportunities to be active participants, including taking leadership roles.

5. **Offer couples counseling at your church.** A commitment to your faith usually means that you are equally committed to the sanctity of marriage and the family.

6. **Open the doors of your sanctuaries to the children and families who need a place to go, a place to be, a secure haven after school, on evenings and weekends, and during holidays.** The church must open its doors. The church must be open every day, not only on Sundays. It should become the focal point of community-based activities and address the urgent social conditions that confront our communities.

7. **Become a volunteer and encourage others to do so as well.** Church volunteers are needed. Retired men and women, college and high school students, and any other willing workers can organize activities to reach out and help the children in the community to have a chance to grow up and to feel that they can be somebody.

8. **Create an after-school learning center.** This will provide youths with a structured place to do their homework and enjoy recreational activities under the supervision of caring volunteers, whether they are high school and college students or senior citizens.

9. **Preach values not only from the pulpit but also in the neighborhoods.** The credible moral voice has traditionally been reserved for our religious leaders. We welcome them to step up to the plate.

10. **Recognize that young people do not like to be preached at but engaged in such a way that we earn their trust.** We have taught them to think independently, and they have no doubt inherited some of our agnosticism about faith and religion. Young people who are skeptical about faith can still believe strongly in service and fellowship. Our churches can become their community centers. They can organize the forums on identity formation and affirmative action. They can rally the troops to help a homeless family and to send petitions to Congress.

# 21

# Timeless Treasures for the State and the Nation

There are a great many things that we must urge state and federal governments to do to strengthen and support our families. Here are a few:

1. **Help create jobs.** Government must create publicly funded job-training programs and public-sector positions. There are many unskilled and unemployed people who are not likely to be trained and hired by the private sector. Government should be the safety net for these individuals. Middle-class families are important advocates for poor families.

2. **Advocate family-friendly policies.** Support candidates for public office at the local, state, and federal levels who have pro-family policies.

3. **Rank cities that are best for families.** Just as local chambers of commerce and other groups rank cities as the best for retirement or as the most "livable," insist that such rankings also evaluate cities for the support they provide for families. Parents will have greater choices as to where to raise their children.

4. **Advocate more open spaces for children.** It appears that fewer and fewer cities organize their space for the use of children and families. Insist that the politicians, zoning boards, and others turn vacant lots and buildings into havens for children and families.

5. **Reward businesses that take leadership.** Businesses should nurture future workers by establishing cooperative programs with schools, churches, and other institutions. The purpose is to socialize youths in the meaning of work and how to get involved with honest work before they graduate from school, and before they become adults.

6. **Initiate major school reforms at the city and state levels.** These include establishing performance-based evaluations and merit awards for teachers and principals; weeding out ineffective teachers; providing more scholarships for poor children to attend private schools; creating charter schools within public school systems (semiautonomous); and developing adult education for parents and job placement for adults through the industry-schools partnerships.

7.  **Repair aging schools and build new ones.**
    School facilities in many urban communities
    across the nation are eroding. Better-equipped
    science and technology labs that will connect
    children with the global community are urgently
    needed to prepare them for the level of com-
    petition they will need to demonstrate in the
    workplace.

8.  **Take the guns away from teenagers.**    It's time
    to disarm our communities. The police can't do
    this alone. They need strong community sup-
    port, concern, and vigilance. One way to pro-
    vide this is by recruiting young people to form
    neighborhood-watch programs as an adjunct
    to similar adult programs.

9.  **Advocate the passage of gun-control legisla-
    tion.**    Guns are too readily available to the
    general public. They frequently end up in the
    hands of those who use them to harm others.

10. **Get the drugs out of the environment.**    Par-
    ents cannot understand how, as the popular
    expression goes, our society can put men and
    women on the moon but cannot get rid of or,
    at a minimum, greatly reduce the influx of
    drugs into our communities. Press your repre-
    sentatives to make this a major priority.

11. **Create decent, affordable housing for families.**
    Children grow better amid decent surroundings.
    Good housing forms the core of wholesome
    neighborhoods. Government should create
    more subsidized housing for needy families,
    and help to ensure the stability of housing for
    others.

# 22

# Facing Tomorrow

I want to return to my earliest question and leave one more for you to ponder as you continue on your journey: How do we strengthen our children's souls? How do we fortify them with a sense of obligation, hope, trust, and a burning desire to achieve? If we fail to answer these questions, we will have failed history. We will have abandoned the mission that was charted for us centuries ago. We will have failed to raise the next generation of doers.

We are blessed with more wealth, more education, more skills than any generation before us. It is our obligation to teach those who are now entering adulthood a sense of responsibility for solving our collective problems. It is our responsibility to use our social and civic clubs, our professional organizations, our churches, our workplaces, and every other institution in our sphere of influence to do our best for our children, protect them all, organize for change, and chart a moral course through even the muddiest waters.

There are never magical, quick-fix solutions to extraordinary problems. So one is tempted to ask, Why do we have to assume responsibility at all? Why shouldn't our nearly grown children, or the government, or other people fix their own problems? But our values teach us that we have to fix them, because anyone else who is trying to do so cannot succeed alone. We have to fix them because we care. We have to fix them because they are also our problems, our kids, our government, and sometimes we ourselves are "the people." We have to be concerned, because whatever affects some children eventually threatens all of them. We have to fix them because we have to ensure that there will be a wholesome and healthy generation of young people to take up the reins after we have stepped aside.

Whether we are aerospace engineers, social workers, teachers, day-care providers, or homemakers, we have to take up the doers' mantle. There is no contradiction between being a good and competent modern professional and being an old-fashioned doer. See what has to be done, and take it on. People who sit back and wait for someone to instruct them on what to do next don't get very far in life. Doers, on the other hand, make life's journey with a firm sense of purpose and identity, reinforced by the knowledge that they have met the challenge, helped themselves, and given back something worthy.

# SELECTED BIBLIOGRAPHY

$F$or children's books that affirm black values, the best resource is *Black Books Galore! Guide to Great African American Children's Books* (John Wiley & Sons, 1998) by Donna Rand, Toni Trent Parker, and Sheila Foster. Your family's library should also include the following classic and contemporary titles:

Angleou, Maya. *I Know Why the Caged Bird Sings* (Bantam Books, 1983).

Baldwin, James. *Go Tell It on the Mountain* (Modern Library, 1995).

Bell, Derrick. *Faces at the Bottom of the Well: The Permanence of Racism* (Basic Books, 1993).

Bennett, Lerone. *Before the Mayflower: A History of Black America* (Johnson Publications, 1988).

Cain, Hope Felder, (editor). *The Original African Heritage Study Bible: King James Version/Black Leatherette* (Winston-Derek Publishing, 1993).

Billingsely, Andrew. *Climbing Jacob's Ladder: The Enduring Legacy of African-American Families* (Touchstone Books, 1994).

Brooks, Gwendolyn. *Selected Poems* (HarperCollins, 1982).

Clinton, Hillary. *It Takes a Village and Other Lessons* (Touchstone Books, 1996).

Comer, James P. *Maggie's American Dream: The Life and Times of a Black Family* (Plume, 1989).

Comer, James P. and Alvin F. Poussaint. *Raising Black Children* (NAL/Dutton, 1992).

Davis, Arthur P., J. Saunders Redding, and Joyce Ann Joyce (editors). *The New Cavalcade: African American Writing from 1760 to the Present,* Vols. I, II (Howard University Press, 1991, 1992).

DuBois, W.E.B. *The Souls of Black Folk* (Bantam Classics, 1989).

Dyson, Michael Eric. *Race Rules: Navigating the Color Line* (Vintage Books, 1997).

Edelman, Marian Wright. *The Measure of Our Success: A Letter to My Children and Yours* (Beacon Press, 1993).

Ellison, Ralph. *Invisible Man.* (Vintage Books, 1994).

Franklin, John Hope. *From Slavery to Freedom: A History of African Americans,* 7th edition (Knopf, 1994).

Gaines, Ernest. *A Gathering of Old Men* (Vintage Books, 1992).

Gates, Henry Louis, Jr., and Nellie Y. McKay (editors). *The Norton Anthology of African American Literature* (W.W. Norton & Company, 1996).

Giddings, Paula. *When and Where I Enter: The Impact of Black Women on Race and Sex in America* (Bantam Books, 1985).

Goss, Linda, and Marian E. Barnes (editors). *Talk That Talk: An Anthology of African American Storytelling* (Touchstone, 1989).

Greene, Bob, and Oprah Winfrey. *Make the Connection: Ten Steps to a Better Body and a Better Life* (Hyperion, 1996).

Haley, Alex. *The Autobiography of Malcolm X* (Ballantine, 1992).

Hansberry, Lorraine. *A Raisin in the Sun* (Vintage Books, 1994).

Hunter-Gault, Charlayne. *In My Place* (Vintage Books, 1993).

McBride, James. *The Color of Water: A Black Man's Tribute to His White Mother* (Riverhead Books, 1997).

Morrison, Toni. *Beloved* (Plume, 1994).

Naylor, Gloria. *The Women of Brewster Place* (Penguin, 1993).

Powell, Colin. *My American Journey* (Ballantine, 1996).

Suskind, Ron. *A Hope in the Unseen: An American Odyssey from the Inner City to the Ivy League* (Broadway Books, 1998).

Taulbert, Clifton L. *Once Upon a Time When We Were Colored* (Penguin, 1995).

Taylor, Susan. *In the Spirit: The Inspirational Writings of Susan L. Taylor* (HarperCollins, 1994).

Vanzant, Iyanla. *Acts of Faith: Daily Meditations for People of Color* (Fireside, 1993).

Vanzant, Iyanla. *One Day My Soul Just Opened Up: 40 Days and 40 Nights Towards Spiritual Strength and Personal Growth* (Fireside, 1998).

Walker, Alice. *The Color Purple* (Pocket Books, 1996).

Walker, Alice. *In Search of Our Mothers' Gardens* (Harcourt Brace Jovanovich, 1983).

Walker, Margaret. *For My People* (Ayer Co. Publications, 1968).

Walker, Margaret. *Jubilee* (Bantam Books, 1984).

Washington, Booker T. *Up from Slavery* (Dover Publications, 1995).

West, Cornell. *Race Matters* (Beacon Press, 1993).

Williams, Patricia J. *The Alchemy of Race and Rights: Diary of a Law Professor* (Harvard University Press, 1991).

# RESOURCES
-- -- --

Thousands of independent groups, programs, and organizations support black values. You can probably find them in your area by contacting your local churches, schools, and community centers. This section lists several leading nationwide resources and practical resource books.

## FAMILY REUNIONS

More than 45 percent of African Americans travel each year to a family reunion. To organize a large-scale reunion takes a huge amount of preparation—from planning attendance to organizing activities, buying gifts, arranging videos, finding space, and writing newsletters. For resource lists and guidance—from locating lost relatives to obtaining park permits, form planning a budget to keeping a recorded history and directory—turn to *The Family Reunion Planner* (Macmillan General Reference, 1997) by Donna Beasley and Donna Carter or other available books.

## FAMILY GENEOLOGY

Thousands of African Americans are studying their genealogies. If you are interested in the topic, contact Heritage Books, 1540E Pointer Ridge Place, Bowie, Maryland 20716. This publishing house specializes in genealogy and offers many titles.

On the Internet, the Afrigeneas mailing list is focused on genealogical research and resources in general and on African ancestry in particular. This web site serves as a focal point for information about genealogical sources worldwide.

Another excellent starting point is Donna Beasley, Donna Carter, and William Haley's *Family Pride: The Complete Guide to Tracing African-American Genealogy* (Macmillian General Reference, 1997). It outlines the resources available to plot one's lineage, from oral history and census reports to church and manumission records, from the National Archives to the Internet, complete with step-by-step instructions on how to conduct the search, gather findings, and publish a finished document.

## HISTORIC SITES

Visiting black historic sites will help bring history to life for children. For a complete guide to 800 places in the National Register of Historic Places that have played a role in black history in 42 states and 2 U.S. territories, I recommend *African American Historic Places,* edited by Beth L. Savage (The Preservation Press, 1994).

Notable family-friendly sites and museums include:

- **The National Civil Rights Museum in Memphis, Tennessee.** This museum is located at the Lorraine Motel, where Dr. Martin Luther King, Jr., was tragically assassinated April 4, 1968.

- **Civil rights monuments in Montgomery, Alabama.** In the state capitol complex stands the Dexter Avenue Baptist Church, a simple brick building where Martin Luther King, Jr., served as pastor from 1954 to 1960 and supporters rallied around Rosa Parks in the Montgomery bus boycott of 1955–56. Around the corner is the Civil Rights Memorial, two blocks west of the state capitol at the entrance to the Southern Poverty Law Center, 400 Washington Avenue. Designed by Vietnam Memorial architect Maya Lin, the monument consists of a circular black granite table inscribed with the names of 40 people killed in struggle. The new Rosa Parks/Bus Boycott Historical Monument is outside the Eureka Theater.

- **Martin Luther King, Jr., Center for Social Change in Atlanta, Georgia.** The King Center was established in 1968 by Mrs. Coretta Scott King as a living memorial dedicated to preserving the legacy of her husband. He is also buried on the site. His birthplace is nearby on Auburn Avenue.

- **African American Civil War Memorial, Washington, D.C.** The number of black troops in the Union Army was larger than the entire Confederate Army in the final months of the war. Located in the historic Shaw district near downtown Washington, the memorial lists the names of two hundred thousand men of African descent who fought in the Civil War.

- **The Underground Railroad.** To commemorate the approximate routes taken by slaves escaping to freedom before the Civil War, numerous preservation sites have been established. For a study guide and further information, contact the web site of the National Park Service.

## TRAINING AND ADVOCACY

To join forces with the National Urban League, the National Association for the Advancement of Colored People (NAACP), or the National Alliance of Black School Educators (NABSE), contact your regional or local affiliate chapter. Other national advocates include:

- **The Children's Defense Fund:** 25 E Street, N.W., Washington, D.C. A strong and effective voice for all the children of America, who cannot vote, lobby, or speak for themselves. They pay particular attention to the needs of poor and minority children and those with disabilities.

- **National Black Child Development Institute:** 1023 15th Street, N.W., Suite 600, Washington, D.C. 20005. The NBCDI has affiliates throughout the country. In addition to its resource center, public policy advocacy, and publications, it hosts a national conference annually.

## SERVICE PROGRAMS

You can count on the YMCA, YWCA, Boy Scouts of America, and Girl Scouts of America for programs that help children develop into mentally healthy, socially competent adults. The following organizations also do a good job in this area:

- **Girls Incorporated:** 30 East 33rd Street, New York, NY 10016-5395. Formerly the Girls Clubs of America, its programs encourage math and science education, pregnancy prevention, media literacy, adolescent health, substance abuse prevention, and sports participation.

- **Boys and Girls Clubs of America:** 1230 W. Peachtree Street, N.W., Atlanta, GA 30309-3447. More than 25 national programs are available. Concerns range from education to the environment, health, the arts, careers, alcohol/drug and pregnancy prevention, gang prevention, leadership development, and athletics.

- **Delta Sigma Theta Sorority, Inc.:** 1707 New Hampshire Avenue N.W., Washington, D.C. 20009. Some 870 local chapters conduct programs for girls such as the Delta Academy, offering educational and personal support. The Delta National Social Action Commission provides updates on national public policy and civil rights activities.

- **Alpha Kappa Alpha Sorority, Inc.:** 5656 S Stony Island Avenue, Chicago, IL 60637. With over 820 local chapters, the oldest black women's sorority launched its Partnership in Mathematics and Science (PIMS) initiative. Activities include AKA International Mathematics and Science Awareness Week, training for educators, and math and science skills camps for students. AKA also sponsors Putting Families FIRST and People's Forums, geared toward how-to information about using existing social services.

- **Zeta Phi Beta Sorority, Inc.:** 1734 New Hampshire Avenue N.W., Washington, D.C. 20009. Through its National Education Foundation, the 500 chapters of Zeta Phi Beta sponsor tutoring, seminars for children, and family literacy activities.

- **Sigma Gamma Rho Sorority, Inc.:** 8800 S Stony Island Avenue, Chicago, IL 60617. Through 400 chapters,

Sigma Gamma Rho offers support and information to young people on subjects ranging from personal finance to coping with AIDS in the family.

- **Alpha Phi Alpha Fraternity, Inc.:** 2313 St. Paul Street, Baltimore MD 21218-5234. **Kappa Alpha Psi Fraternity, Inc.:** 2322-24 N Broad Street, Philadelphia PA 19132-4590. **Omega Psi Phi Fraternity, Inc.:** 2714 Georgia Avenue, N.W., Washington, D.C. **Phi Beta Sigma Fraternity, Inc.:** 145 Kennedy Street, N.W., Washington D.C. 20011. All, including college alumni chapters, are dedicated to working with young men, particularly in the college-age group.

- **Concerned Black Men:** Founded by a group of policemen in Philadelphia, a dozen chapters in urban areas mentor young black boys.

- **100 Black Men of America:** 127 Peachtree Street, N.E., Atlanta, GA 30309. Chapters nationwide offer mentoring, antiviolence, and job programs as well as sustain partnerships with public schools.

- **National Coalition of 100 Black Women:** 300 Park Avenue, 17th Floor, New York, NY 10022. The Coalition of 100 Black Women is a national organization with chapters in several major cities. It promotes self-esteem programs for girls and take-a-girl-to-work day, among other activities.

- **The National Council of Negro Women, Inc.:** 1211 Connecticut Avenue, N.W., Room 702, Washington, D.C. Thirty-four affiliated national women's public service sororities, business and professional women's associations, women's societies, civic groups, women's fraternal orders, and civil rights organizations under the NCNW umbrella reach more than 4 million women, with an extended outreach of at least 5.5 million when including international affiliations. Programs include the NCNW Black Family Reunion Celebrations. Its publications include *The Black Family Dinner Quilt Cookbook* (Simon & Schuster, 1994) and *Mother Africa's Table* (Doubleday, 1998).

# INDEX OF INSPIRATIONAL THEMES AND VIRTUES